EFFECTIVE
EDGE

How Christians Today Can Accomplish the Lord's Work

Gregory Alan Tidwell

Editor of *Gospel Advocate*

GOSPEL
ADVOCATE

A TRUSTED NAME SINCE 1855

Published by Gospel Advocate Co.
1006 Elm Hill Pike, Nashville, TN 37210
www.gospeladvocate.com

ISBN: 978-0-89225-648-8

TABLE *of* CONTENTS

FOREWORD

We have learned to honor successful people, but we have learned to admire even more those who are effective. Those who know their skills and hone them to achieve the greatest usefulness demand our recognition and appreciation.

Gregory Alan Tidwell, editor of the *Gospel Advocate*, focuses his attention and ours too in *The Effective Edge: How Christians Today Can Accomplish the Lord's Work*, a study on using our talents, skills and opportunities to achieve the most meaningful results.

Although this study is aimed at the Christian who seeks to be effective in all areas of life and service, Tidwell draws bountifully from biblical examples, directions and injunctions. At the same time, he supplements with meaningful and useful illustrations from all phases of human experience. Ample references are made to bestsellers, advice gurus, politicians, poets and preachers, whose words add spice to each subject. Tidwell also draws effectively from his own wide range of personal experiences from student days, community participation and church involvement.

The audience for this book is everybody. With chapters devoted to multiple areas that require the Christian to be effective, Tidwell deals with topics such as leadership, example-setting, goal-setting, stewardship and planning. His assessments of current situations in the church are astute, and his solutions for these problems are valid and workable.

To evaluate our own levels of effectiveness in all the areas of a Christian's life demands a careful study of God's Word. James described the Bible as a mirror where we can see ourselves in order to inspect our spiritual appearance. Like a good mirror, God's Word reveals us as we are. But if, in James' words, we see ourselves and then go away, forgetting the kind of person we saw, we deprive ourselves of God's richest blessings (James 1:23-25).

The standard for doing our best in loving God and others is best revealed in the life of Jesus and the teachings of His apostles. Paul's very brief letter to Philemon offers encouragement to its recipient by telling him of Paul's prayers for him: "I thank my God, making mention of you always in my prayers" (v. 4 NKJV). Then Paul identified some of the blessings he prayed for.

Included in those entreaties is this: "that the sharing of your faith may become *effective* by the acknowledgment of every good thing which is in you in Christ Jesus" (Philemon 6 NKJV, emphasis added). Paul prayed for Philemon to gain an "effective edge." In this study, Tidwell encourages each reader to seek his own.

– Dennis Loyd
Gospel Advocate Associate Editor

INTRODUCTION & ACKNOWLEDGMENTS

"Whatever you do, work heartily, as for the Lord and not for men," Paul wrote in Colossians, "knowing that from the Lord you will receive the inheritance as your reward. You are serving the Lord Christ" (3:23-24). As Christians, we are called to follow the Savior in an awesome and important work. Our effectiveness in this work is important because of what is at stake: our souls and the souls of others.

"For it is time for judgment to begin at the household of God; and if it begins with us, what will be the outcome for those who do not obey the gospel of God?" Peter warned. "And 'If the righteous is scarcely saved, what will become of the ungodly and the sinner?' " (1 Peter 4:17-18). In response to the importance of our work, this study highlights practices to enhance personal and congregational effectiveness.

Sources for This Study

The framework of this book is a conviction of the inspiration and authority of Scripture. Everything I have written rests on this understanding. At the coronation of Queen Elizabeth II, she was handed a Bible with these words:

> Our gracious Queen: to keep your Majesty ever mind-
> ful of the Law and the Gospel of God as the Rule for
> the whole life and government of Christian Princes,
> we present you with this Book, the most valuable thing
> that this world affords. Here is Wisdom; This is the royal
> Law; These are the lively Oracles of God.

Just so, we should revere Scripture. The Bible is the final guide
to effectiveness in the Lord's church and in all of life.

My understanding of Scripture and its effective application has
been shaped by the example of faith modeled by men who have
served as leaders among churches of Christ. Through my association with the Gospel Advocate Co., I have been privileged to know
or to know of men who accomplished much by what they enabled
others to do in the Lord's service. This heritage of faith that began
with Tolbert Fanning continues in the life and work of the *Gospel
Advocate*'s current publisher, Neil Anderson.

The influence of other leaders in the church, who have gone to
their reward, is evident in what I have written. Jim Bill McInteer
was my preacher and mentor, while Batsell Barrett Baxter made an
indelible impression on me as my teacher at Lipscomb University.
Although my association with Ira North was more limited, his influence on my thinking was huge, especially through his book *Balance.*

My major professor at Vanderbilt University, the late Herman
Norton, helped me to understand the importance of historical
analysis in seeing patterns of effective work. My advisor at Ohio
State University, Llyle J. Barker Jr., taught me much about servant
leadership. Both of these men retired from distinguished military
careers to take on continued service as college professors.

Thanks and Remembrance

One of my greatest blessings in life is the memory of my parents,
Cam and Hazel Tidwell. Having gone to be with the Lord, I know
we will be together again.

My wife, Peggy, and our sons, David and Jordan, have sup-
ported me in every good work. Without my loving family, this
book would never have been written.

I must also thank Phil Sanders, who has served as my confidant
and collaborator throughout the past 20 years; Justin Rogers,
Will Hanstein, Dewayne Bryant and Chad Ramsey, scholars who

combine intellect with faithfulness; and Matthew Morine, who reminds me that faith is a journey best traveled with a friend.

My appreciation for the extended family of the Gospel Advocate Co. knows no bounds. Especially, in the production of this book, I must thank the skilled editorial team led by Dennis Loyd and Debra G. Wright.

Finally, I must acknowledge the contribution and support of two friends, without whom this book would never have been written: Walt Wallingford and Kerry Anderson. More than 15 years ago, Walt encouraged me to write a book. Although he did not live to read this volume, much in its pages reflects his influence.

Kerry did read my manuscript and helped me refine its focus. His suggestions were on target and enhanced what I had written. This book was in production at the time of his unexpected death. Kerry had a rare gift of insight and the ability to see through the clutter of life. His dedication to the Lord's service continues in the work of the Gospel Advocate Co.

Many thanks to all,

Gregory Alan Tidwell
Gospel Advocate Editor

1

Why Study CHRISTIAN *Effectiveness?*

Effectiveness is in short supply. In the church, as in government and business, the lack of effectiveness hinders our success and limits the good we can accomplish.

Often, when faced with failure, we seek an easy scapegoat rather than deal with the hard task of owning up to problems in our thoughts and actions. We imagine if only we had more resources, knew the latest methods, or were free from certain obstacles, then we would succeed. Blaming circumstances, however, misses the mark. We must look deeper. We must look at ourselves and, with honesty, face our own failures.

The problems we face as Christians do not come primarily from external threats or from a lack of resources. God has given us everything we need to succeed. As Paul wrote, "God is able to make all grace abound to you, so that having all sufficiency in all things at all times, you may abound in every good work" (2 Corinthians 9:8).

What an overwhelming abundance we have received as Christians. Yet do we "abound in every good work"? In many circumstances, the work of the church is abandoned rather than abounding. We can inventory wonderful opportunities, but too often, we see opportunities pass us by.

God has provided everything we need for success. Yet we are

failing to succeed. Our failure comes from mishandling the talents, resources and opportunities God has provided. We are failing as stewards, which also means we are failing in the work of the Lord, for our work in His service is stewardship.

Selfishness Vs. Stewardship

We are failing in effective service, in part, because we are failing in our relationships with one another. We have forgotten how to relate to one another because we have forgotten how to relate to God. "Whatever disunites man from God," British statesman Edmund Burke observed, "also disunites man from man."

We see effects of disunity in problems facing our society. The disintegration of the American family, the fear of violent crime, the uncertainty of economic change, and the increasing polarization of the political process all spring from the same source. The problems we face as a nation are symptoms of selfishness working against the common good. We are no longer looking out for one another because we are no longer looking up to God.

We are no longer looking out for one another because we are no longer looking up to God.

The effects of disunity are also present in problems we face in the church. The travesty of "entertainment worship," the lack of doctrinal convictions, the moral looseness, and the pervasive apathy plaguing our congregations all spring from the same source. The problems we face in the church are symptoms of selfishness that neither honors God nor serves other people. Selfishness corrupts the freedom we have in Christ, as Paul warned:

> For you were called to freedom, brothers. Only do not use your freedom as an opportunity for the flesh, but through love serve one another. For the whole law is fulfilled in one word: "You shall love your neighbor as yourself." But if you bite and devour one another, watch out that you are not consumed by one another. (Galatians 5:13-15)

Historically, people have realized that civilization requires restraint and that effectiveness requires subordinating selfish interests for the common good. In contrast, the modern "do your own thing" approach weakens the social fabric and makes real effectiveness impossible. From a standpoint of selfishness, there can be manipulation and intimidation, but there cannot be real effectiveness.

Unified Effort Through a Unified Faith

Effectiveness requires a shared commitment to a common goal. This shared commitment binds people together and provides a framework within which effective service can occur. Within the church, our shared commitment should be a shared submission to the will of God.

People seek out positions of power and influence in the church for a wide range of reasons. Some, selfishly, seek power to advance private agendas.

A self-centered approach, however, undercuts the very idea of meaning in religion. Exercising power in the church for superficial reasons ends up being ineffectual manipulation. The example of Christ guides us to never seek merely to please ourselves; rather, effectiveness in Christian service has as its primary mission to be pleasing to God. That is to say, an effective Christian believes and obeys what God says in Scripture.

Christian effectiveness presupposes an authentic Christian commitment shared by members of the church. The principles and techniques outlined in the following chapters can only enhance Christian effectiveness in the context of a shared commitment to the authority of Jesus Christ. Without such a commitment, Christian effectiveness cannot exist.

> *Effectiveness requires a shared commitment to a common goal.*

What Our Study Hopes to Accomplish

What benefit will this series of lessons be in a personal quest for greater effectiveness? Let's consider what can be expected throughout this study.

First, in this study is an outline of methods that will help increase effectiveness in every area of life. The concepts we will consider have application in business and family life as well as in a congregational setting.

Second, through this study learning tools are provided that will help cultivate the abilities of other people. These will help them develop into the men and women of faith God has called them to be. This principle is the center of servant leadership:

to build other people up, enabling them to be more than what they were before.

Third, and most important, this study is designed as a tool that will help examine our responsibility before God, as the Lord's servants, and to enhance our faithful service in the church. Actions speak louder than words.

For REFLECTION

1. *Define "effectiveness."*

2. *Can a bad man or woman be an effective person?*

3. *How is effectiveness in the church different from effectiveness in business, athletics or the military? How is it the same?*

4. *Name a person definitely considered to be effective. Why is he or she effective?*

NOTES: _____

_____

_____

_____

_____

_____

_____

_____

_____

_____

_____

_____

_____

_____

_____

_____

_____

_____

_____

_____

2

Effective LEADERSHIP

Considering Christian effectiveness, we need to consider two topics concerning leadership in the church. After all, as former U.S. Secretary of State Henry Kissinger noted, "If you do not know where you are going, every road will get you nowhere." Who, then, is a leader, and how do we understand leadership in the church?

Think of a great leader of the past century. What name immediately comes to mind? Perhaps Winston Churchill, who inspired millions of people to resist German aggression. Or Adolf Hitler, who inspired millions of people to embrace the Nazi vision. What about Ronald Reagan, the "Great Communicator," or Margaret Thatcher, the "Iron Lady," who led the Western democracies in thwarting Soviet aggression? Or Joseph Stalin and Mao Zedong, the Communists dictators who murdered untold millions of their people while ruling their respective countries?

What separates a Churchill from a Hitler, or a Thatcher from a Stalin? Each was a person of great political power, but one central difference made Churchill admirable and Hitler detestable. The difference between a leader and a tyrant is the moral focus that guides a leader's actions. Lacking a moral standard, it is not possible for true leadership to exist.

As Stephen R. Covey, in his book *The 7 Habits of Highly Effective*

People, remarked: "Management is efficiency in climbing the ladder of success; leadership determines whether the ladder is leaning against the right wall." Fascists, communists and gangsters are often skilled managers of power, but their ladders are leaning against the wrong walls. Lacking correct moral vision, they fail in the only meaningful test of effectiveness: the effect of one's influence in the lives of followers.

Leadership is more than power. Leadership is influence for good.

President John Quincy Adams described this quality: "If your actions inspire others to dream more, learn more, do more and become more, you are a leader." From this point of view, leadership is more than power. Leadership is influence for good. Every effective Christian exercises leadership in that he or she enhances others in Christian service.

A leader is someone at the forefront of understanding and action, someone who charts the course others will follow. True leadership is often hidden and subtle in the present, only later showing itself. Ultimately, the full measure of a leader's influence can only be assessed with the consideration of eternity.

A Framework for Leadership

Faith, then, is an essential first step in understanding real leadership. From a Christian perspective, God's revealed truth provides the moral framework within which we can build an understanding of effective leadership. Paul described this framework of understanding in 1 Corinthians 15:50-58:

> I tell you this, brothers: flesh and blood cannot inherit the kingdom of God, nor does the perishable inherit the imperishable. Behold! I tell you a mystery. We shall not all sleep, but we shall all be changed, in a moment, in the twinkling of an eye, at the last trumpet. For the trumpet will sound, and the dead will be raised imperishable, and we shall be changed. For this perishable body must put on the imperishable, and this mortal body must put on immortality. When the perishable puts on the imperishable, and the mortal puts on immortality, then shall come to pass the saying that is written: "Death is swallowed up in victory." "O death, where is your victory? O death, where is your

sting?" The sting of death is sin, and the power of sin is the law. But thanks be to God, who gives us the victory through our Lord Jesus Christ. Therefore, my beloved brothers, be steadfast, immovable, always abounding in the work of the Lord, knowing that in the Lord your labor is not in vain.

Building our understanding of leadership with a view toward eternity, Christians must rely on the truths of Scripture as a foundation for effective leadership. While the world may challenge our insistence on the Bible, we are sure God knows best how the church is to operate. Two topics, in particular, from a distinctively Christian understanding of leadership should be considered: male spiritual leadership and servant leadership. Let's briefly consider these topics in the light of Scripture.

Male Spiritual Leadership

The Bible stresses a special place of leadership for Christian men both in the home and in the church. While recognizing the appropriateness of women exercising influence and direction in certain contexts, the clear teaching of Scripture distinguishes between the responsibilities of men and women. The distinct nature of male spiritual leadership is assumed throughout the Bible and directly stated in several indisputable passages.

Scripture teaches male spiritual leadership in the home in Ephesians 5:22-24:

Wives, submit to your own husbands, as to the Lord. For the husband is the head of the wife even as Christ is the head of the church, his body, and is himself its Savior. Now as the church submits to Christ, so also wives should submit in everything to their husbands.

Whatever else may be said to qualify this text, Paul described an order in the home. The husband is to lead, and the wife is to submit. Passages such as Colossians 3:18 and 1 Peter 3:1 echo this teaching.

Male spiritual leadership is also a pattern designed by God for the ordering of the church. Implicitly, the exclusively male composition of the apostles (Matthew 10:2-4) and the requirement of elders and of deacons to be husbands (1 Timothy 3:2, 12) show this truth. Another prohibition against women leading in public teaching in the church is even more direct:

Let a woman learn quietly with all submissiveness. I do not permit a woman to teach or to exercise authority over a man; rather, she is to remain quiet. For Adam was formed first, then Eve; and Adam was not deceived, but the woman was deceived and became a transgressor. (1 Timothy 2:11-14)

Paul was clear. Women are not "to teach or to exercise authority over a man." They are not to do so because of the order in which God created Adam and Eve and because of how they fell into sin. Rooting these prohibitions in the truth of creation, Paul showed they are valid for Christians in all places and all times. The principle of male spiritual leadership is in place. First Corinthians 14:34-35 makes the same point:

The women should keep silent in the churches. For they are not permitted to speak, but should be in submission, as the Law also says. If there is anything they desire to learn, let them ask their husbands at home. For it is shameful for a woman to speak in church.

> *All members of the church, both men and women, are to serve one another effectively through the gifts provided by God.*

The prohibition against women speaking in worship in no way lessens the shared responsibility of all Christians to engage in the work of the church. Scripture commands all members of the church, both men and women, to serve one another effectively through the gifts provided by God (1 Peter 4:10), and this service is necessary for the life and growth of the church (1 Corinthians 12:12-26). In many contexts, women will exercise a form of leadership, both in the home and in the church. This service, however, must never blur the distinct spiritual leadership God has reserved for men.

Servant Leadership

Often, Christians are at odds with the prevailing trends of society. One striking exception is the increasing acceptance among management theorists of the distinctively Christian idea of "servant leadership." Beginning with Robert K. Greenleaf, who published *The Servant as Leader* in 1970, many popular management writers have embraced the value of this approach.

Unlike a top-down hierarchical approach, servant leadership stresses teamwork, conviction, understanding and the ethical use of power. The leader is a servant first, making the mindful choice to lead in order to better serve others. This method has become widespread, and today, successful leadership is defined as influence, not power.

Servant leadership has become fashionable, yet the idea is still out of step with much leadership thinking of the past. Jesus recognized this exceptionally when He told His disciples:

> You know that those who are considered rulers of the Gentiles lord it over them, and their great ones exercise authority over them. But it shall not be so among you. But whoever would be great among you must be your servant, and whoever would be first among you must be slave of all. For even the Son of Man came not to be served but to serve, and to give his life as a ransom for many. (Mark 10:42-45)

Following the example of Jesus, Christians approach leadership from an outlook of consideration rather than from a perspective of conceit. Paul used this example to encourage compliance from his readers:

> Have this mind among yourselves, which is yours in Christ Jesus, who, though he was in the form of God, did not count equality with God a thing to be grasped, but emptied himself, by taking the form of a servant, being born in the likeness of men. And being found in human form, he humbled himself by becoming obedient to the point of death, even death on a cross. (Philippians 2:5-8)

For Christians, servant leadership is more than a passing management fad. The example of Jesus Christ calls us to embrace a mindset of service. His example, however, places a different spin on service. Servant leadership, in the context of management theory, places other people before oneself. The Christian outlook, however, takes humility one step further by incorporating the idea of obedience to God. Without this ultimate reference point, servant leadership can sink into a tyranny of the many replacing the tyranny of the one. Recognizing our shared duty to follow the will of God, Christians have a framework within which genuine leadership can occur.

For REFLECTION

1. *How does a proper view of the inspiration and authority of Scripture shape one's leadership style?*

2. *What is the relationship between stewardship and leadership?*

3. *When should a leader listen to his followers, and when should the followers be told what to do?*

4. *What do you think is the most important skill to possess as a Christian leader?*

NOTES: _____

_____

_____

_____

_____

_____

_____

_____

_____

_____

_____

_____

_____

_____

_____

_____

_____

_____

3

Effective
EXAMPLE-SETTING

I love collecting rare books, especially autographed copies from famous authors. In addition to volumes signed by five presidents of the U.S., I have volumes autographed by world leaders such as Henry Kissinger and Margaret Thatcher. Shortly before Sir Edmund Hillary's death in 2008, I obtained a signed edition of his memoir, *View From the Summit.*

Sir Edmund is a fascinating figure. Serving with distinction in the Royal New Zealand Air Force during World War II, he went on to become renowned as a philanthropist and adventurer. With a life adorned by many accomplishments, he is best remembered as the first man confirmed to reach the summit of Mount Everest.

As the world's highest mountain, Everest rises 29,029 feet above sea level. This altitude challenges climbers with high winds, reduced oxygen and frigid temperatures. For decades, teams had attempted an ascent, only to be turned back. Sir Edmund succeeded in reaching the summit through discipline, skill and determination.

Sir Edmund triumphed in scaling the mountain, but more to the point, he showed how something that had never been done before could be accomplished. Other climbers followed his example, and by the end of the 2008 climbing season, there had been 4,102 ascents to the summit by about 2,700 individuals. Such is the influence of an inspiring example.

The power of Sir Edmund's enabling example for mountain climbers serves as a reminder to anyone seeking to be a leader. The best way to engender excellence in others is to embody excellence in one's self.

Example is important for effectiveness in every area of life. Aristotle outlined the three modes of persuasion and placed one's ethical standing and example above all else. In the business world, the example of the individuals heading major corporations sets the tone for all who work there. In the church, as well, an essential aspect of service is the example we set for others coupled with the ability to follow the examples of faith God has given us. Learning by example is integral to being a disciple.

Learning From Biblical Examples

The Bible teaches many truths through biography, showing some examples we should follow and showing other examples we should avoid. The destruction of Sodom and Gomorrah, according to 2 Peter 2:6, provides "an example of what is going to happen to the ungodly," while James 5:10 displays the Old Testament prophets "as an example of suffering and patience." The greatest example provided in Scripture, of course, is the life of our Savior, detailed in the four Gospels.

> *The best way to engender excellence in others is to embody excellence in one's self.*

Jesus Christ, the Son of God, is our perfect example. Showing the way of humble service in washing the feet of His disciples, Christ explained the point of this lesson in John 13:15: "For I have given you an example, that you also should do just as I have done to you." Our Savior also provided an example of patient endurance, as 1 Peter 2:21 encourages: "For to this you have been called, because Christ also suffered for you, leaving you an example, so that you might follow in his steps."

Beyond these direct references to the example of Christ, we find in Scripture a pattern of obedient faith displayed by Jesus as He lived and worked among men. Detailing the full impact of this example, John wrote:

My little children, I am writing these things to you so that you may not sin. But if anyone does sin, we have an advocate with the Father, Jesus Christ the righteous. He is the propitiation for our sins, and not for ours only but also for the sins of the whole world. And by this we know that we have come to know him, if we keep his commandments. Whoever says "I know him" but does not keep his commandments is a liar, and the truth is not in him, but whoever keeps his word, in him truly the love of God is perfected. By this we may know that we are in him: whoever says he abides in him ought to walk in the same way in which he walked. (1 John 2:1-6)

Obedient faith is the key to walking in the steps of the Savior. Receiving the blessings of His sacrificial death, we should emulate the obedience of His faithful life.

Current Examples
of Christian Excellence

"Example is the school of mankind, and they will learn at no other," Edmund Burke, 18th-century Irish political philosopher, rightly observed. In Scripture we have examples that engage us and move us forward in Christian excellence, but we are also blessed with godly examples in the church today. "Brothers, join in imitating me," Paul wrote in Philippians 3:17, "and keep your eyes on those who walk according to the example you have in us." Not only in Christ and the apostles but in all faithful Christians we can see a pattern of spiritual excellence that serves as our guide.

This pattern of spiritual excellence transcends generations. To the young evangelist Timothy, Paul wrote: "Let no one despise you for your youth, but set the believers an example in speech, in conduct, in love, in faith, in purity" (1 Timothy 4:12). On the other end of the spectrum, Peter instructed:

So I exhort the elders among you, as a fellow elder and a witness of the sufferings of Christ, as well as a partaker in the glory that is going to be revealed: shepherd the flock of God that is among you, exercising oversight, not under compulsion, but willingly, as God would have you; not for shameful gain, but eagerly; not domineering over those in your charge, but being examples to the flock. And when the chief Shepherd appears, you will receive the unfading crown of glory. (1 Peter 5:1-4)

At each stage of our lives, we as Christians should build one another up through the power of the examples we set. Christians of every age have blessed me through their godly examples. One of my joys in ministry is working with teenagers as they begin their journeys of faith. The conviction and sincerity of these young people are refreshing as we see the Lord build His church through their obedient faith. The examples of peers and the examples of older brethren have also inspired me in Christian service.

Men and women of faith provide a great legacy that strengthens the Lord's work long after they have gone to their reward.

Examples have the power to reach across generations. In the sixth grade at David Lipscomb Elementary School, my teacher, Gertrude Deese, often spoke of her grandfather, James A. Harding. Almost a century after his death, Harding's example of faith continues to speak to me. This is the lengthening shadow of example described in Joshua 24:31: "Israel served the LORD all the days of Joshua, and all the days of the elders who outlived Joshua and had known all the work that the LORD did for Israel." Through faith, we are building for eternity.

In Revelation 14:13, John wrote: " 'Blessed are the dead who die in the Lord from now on.' 'Blessed indeed,' says the Spirit, 'that they may rest from their labors, for their deeds follow them!' " Men and women of faith, through their examples, provide a great legacy that strengthens the Lord's work long after they have gone to their reward. This power to reach across the years is an encouragement for us to invest ourselves in the lives of Christians today.

Example Requires Engagement

As a youth, one of my daily rituals was reading the "Peanuts" cartoon in the newspaper. Charles Schulz was my hero. In one cartoon, he showed Lucy berating Linus for not loving mankind, to which Linus replied: "I love mankind ... it's people I can't stand."

Effective Christians must realize influence cannot occur in

isolation. We cannot serve the church without engaging individual Christians. Example requires engagement.

William Croswell Doane, an American bishop of the Episcopal church in the late 19th century, addressed this need for engagement in his poem "The Preacher's Mistake":

The parish priest
Of austerity,
Climbed up in a high church steeple
To be nearer God,
So that he might hand
His word down to His people.

When the sun was high,
When the sun was low,
The good man sat unheeding
Sublunary things.
From transcendency
He was forever reading.

And now and again
When he heard the creak
Of the weather vane a-turning,
He closed his eyes
And said, "Of a truth
From God I now am learning."

And in sermon script
He daily wrote
What he thought was sent from heaven,
And he dropped this down
On his people's heads
Two times one day in seven.

In his age God said,
"Come down and die!"
And he cried out from the steeple,
"Where art thou, Lord?"
And the Lord replied,
"Down here among my people."

Christians should consider the opportunity to serve God's people as an opportunity to serve the Lord. As Jesus reminded us in Matthew 25:40, "I say to you, as you did it to one of the least of these my brothers, you did it to me." The care we exercise in setting the right example in the church is an extension of our loving service to Christ.

Three Ways to Enhance Our Example

While we cannot reduce the example we set to a short checklist, let me propose three areas we should consider in being the example of faith that Christ would want us to be.

Consider How Others See You

An effective Christian must always place the needs of others ahead of his or her personal needs. This priority requires paying attention to the image we project to others. A part of our image is our personal appearance. As we will see in chapter 11, how we present ourselves through our appearance affects the influence we have on others.

Beyond personal appearance, in almost every action we take there will be an influence on others exerted by our example. When we teach a Bible class, visit the sick, or participate in any of the works of the church, we are not only doing good by teaching, visiting and working, but we are doing even more good by influencing other Christians to teach, visit and work.

Maintain Your Integrity

Nobody is perfect, and no one has ever set a perfect example except for our Savior. Recognizing our shortcomings, the integrity with which we live as Christians will, in large part, determine the scope of our influence.

The integrity with which we live as Christians will determine the scope of our influence.

Integrity is especially important in the example we set for younger Christians. Growing older, we become more aware of our own failings and, often, more forgiving of the failures of others. Idealistic youths, however, need to be sheltered from the harsh reality of life's inconsistencies. The standard we should seek in our lives is a seamless obedience to the will of God. Where we inevitably fall short, our example will be compromised.

Manage Your Attitude

Viktor E. Frankl, reflecting on his experience in a German concentration camp in *Man's Search for Meaning,* observed one freedom the Nazis could not take away: "the last of human freedoms – the ability to choose one's attitude in a given set of circumstances."

Far too often we focus on the external world of circumstances that is beyond our control and ignore the internal world of our disposition that we can control. True effectiveness comes from the convictions of the heart, and an authentic example of effectiveness comes from a heart that is in step with the Spirit of God.

Paul described what it means to walk with the Spirit as he described the fruit that the Spirit produces in our lives: "But the fruit of the Spirit is love, joy, peace, patience, kindness, goodness, faithfulness, gentleness, self-control; against such things there is no law" (Galatians 5:22-23).

Notice the attitudinal nature of true spirituality. Notice also the importance of relationships as the venue within which Christian conviction is displayed. For example, a person cannot be kind except in a relationship with someone else.

In his poem "Sermons We See," Edgar A. Guest penned this memorable refrain: "I'd rather see a sermon than hear one any day." With a heart convicted by God's truth, a life directed consistently by this truth, and a consideration of how displaying this truth influences others, we will lead with effective examples – not merely by what we say or do but, more important, by who we are.

For
REFLECTION

1. *Other than Jesus', whose example in Scripture is most meaningful to you? Why?*

2. *What older Christian has influenced you most through his or her example? What does this person inspire you to do?*

3. *How can we avoid the temptations of pride and hypocrisy in using ourselves as examples for others?*

4. *What are the challenges and opportunities we have in setting an example for younger Christians?*

NOTES: _____

_____

_____

_____

_____

_____

_____

_____

_____

_____

_____

_____

_____

_____

_____

_____

Effective
GOAL-SETTING

❝Follow your bliss," pop philosopher Joseph Campbell advised, embodying the "do your own thing" attitude dominating Western thought and culture since the 1960s. The result of this fractured and self-serving approach has been devastating. With each person following his individual desires, the fabric of our lives has unraveled.

In place of this direction-less approach of disintegration, we need a unifying vision of integration. We need a common direction provided by a shared destination. The idea of effectiveness is getting someone somewhere. With this in mind, the purpose of an effective Christian, then, is both to identify the end and the best way to get there.

The Beginning and the End

Peter described those who willfully disregard the beginning and the end:

> For they deliberately overlook this fact, that the heavens existed long ago, and the earth was formed out of water and through water by the word of God, and that by means of these the world that then existed was

deluged with water and perished. But by the same word the heavens and earth that now exist are stored up for fire, being kept until the day of judgment and destruction of the ungodly. (2 Peter 3:5-7)

It is no accident the "do your own thing" approach exists in tandem with a rejection of creation. Believing God was at the beginning in creation entails knowing He will be there at the end in judgment. Contemporary secular thought, with its direction-less design of self-determining freedom, rebels against the constraints of this framework.

I had a little oscar fish imaginatively named "Oscar." More intelligent than most residents of an aquarium, Oscars soon learn to recognize their owners and can even be trained to do basic tricks. I could hold a small morsel of food above Oscar's tank, and he could jump 4 to 5 inches out of the water to snatch it. The children of the congregation would gather outside my office before worship to see Oscar perform. It was like Sea World.

A knowledge of God tells us where we come from and where we are going.

Unfortunately, training a fish to jump is not prudent when there is no cover on the aquarium. One morning, I arrived to find Oscar's dry body on the carpet next to his tank. He found freedom from the constraints of his aquarium, but he had only managed to free himself from that which made his life possible.

In just this way, when people reject the constraints of a life lived with God, they are jumping out of a life-giving context into the destruction of the void. "They promise them freedom, but they themselves are slaves of corruption. For whatever overcomes a person, to that he is enslaved" (2 Peter 2:19).

Believing the Bible, Christians know that God was at the beginning and will be at the end. This information frames our existence and offers a point of integration, providing value and direction for our lives. Being right with God is not merely a part of life; God is the context within which "we live and move and have our being" (Acts 17:28). A knowledge of God tells us where we come from, where we are going, and how we can safely arrive at our final destination.

The early chapters of Genesis set the stage for understanding the world in which we live. Sometimes we assume we can start from nature and come to know God. The revelation provided in nature, however, is fragmented. Looking at the order and beauty of the universe, we well may come to know God's power and wisdom. But what can nature tell us of God's love, mercy and grace?

Sometimes we sing "Have you ever looked at the sunset? … then I say, you've seen Jesus my Lord." It is beautiful poetry, but it is not exactly true. A person could look at the sun rise and set for a thousand years and never know Jesus and His way of salvation. We would never know Jesus loves us, except the Bible tells us so. Looking then into "the sacred writings, which are able to make you wise for salvation" (2 Timothy 3:15), we can find God's mission and how we and those we lead fit into this divine program.

All for His Glory

Through Scripture, we come to know the truth of our creation and the purpose behind it. God, speaking through Isaiah, described the creation of the human race as being for the purpose of His glory:

> I will say to the north, Give up, and to the south, Do not withhold; bring my sons from afar and my daughters from the end of the earth, everyone who is called by my name, whom I created for my glory, whom I formed and made. (Isaiah 43:6-7)

Likewise, in the doxology of Revelation 4:11, God's creation was shown to exist for His glory: "Worthy are you, our Lord and God, to receive glory and honor and power, for you created all things, and by your will they existed and were created."

To glorify God in all we do is the ultimate goal of our existence; for this purpose we were created. "His divine power has granted to us all things that pertain to life and godliness," 2 Peter 1:3 promises, "through the knowledge of him who called us to his own glory and excellence."

The ultimate goal of our existence is to glorify God in all we do.

This understanding of our creation shows the purpose of our existence and helps us define who we are and what God expects us to do. This purpose informs and directs the goals we set for ourselves and for those we lead.

Goals That Glorify God

As we set goals for ourselves and for our service in the kingdom, the ultimate goal of glorifying God establishes a framework guiding us and empowering us to achieve all God wants us to do. Consider, specifically, how a proper focus on the glory of God guides us in benchmarking our evangelistic outreach, Christian service, and godly worship.

Evangelistic Outreach

"Who can utter the mighty deeds of the LORD," Psalm 106:2 asks, "or declare all of his praise?" Our God has done great things; recounting these is the basis of the praise we offer to His glory. We ought to thank God for all of His blessings, and as we remember what He has done for us, we glorify His name.

One work, however, stands out above all that God has ever done. As grand and glorious as the many works of God are, all others pale to the unsurpassable work of salvation He accomplished through His Son.

We glorify God as we live out this salvation in our lives and as we share this salvation with others. Evangelistic outreach is intrinsically an act that glorifies God, as Paul wrote, "so that as grace extends to more and more people it may increase thanksgiving, to the glory of God" (2 Corinthians 4:15). This process of outreach that glorifies God was prophesied in Habakkuk 2:14: "For the earth will be filled with the knowledge of the glory of the LORD as the waters cover the sea."

In my youth, I was aboard an ocean liner, enjoying a family vacation in the Caribbean. One night, out of sight from land, I watched the full moon reflecting on the waves that stretched in every direction. "Water, water everywhere," just as Samuel Taylor Coleridge wrote in "The Rime of the Ancient Mariner." In the same way water covers the sea, God wants knowledge of His glory to cover the earth, and we should want what God wants. This is the evangelistic imperative.

As we assess our priorities and as we set our goals, it is good to glorify God through His gospel – the gift of God's Son. The good news of Jesus Christ, lived in our lives and shared in the world, is our absolute standard. This metric measures the success of our effectiveness beyond anything else we may achieve.

Christian Service

The church is the body of Christ. Service to the Lord's people is service to the Lord. The God of heaven is not "served by human hands, as though He needed anything" (Acts 17:25). "If I were hungry, I would not tell you," God said in Psalm 50:12, "for the world and its fullness are mine." But God's people get hungry. Meeting their needs is service to God.

All the good we do glorifies God. "In the same way, let your light shine before others," Jesus commanded in Matthew 5:16, "so that they may see your good works and give glory to your Father who is in heaven." Yet Scripture places a priority on the good we do within the family of God: "So then, as we have opportunity, let us do good to everyone, and especially to those who are of the household of faith" (Galatians 6:10).

Through God's people being served, God is served. But we must remember God is the One who gives us the gifts through which we serve God's people:

> As each has received a gift, use it to serve one another, as good stewards of God's varied grace: whoever speaks, as one who speaks oracles of God; whoever serves, as one who serves by the strength that God supplies – in order that in everything God may be glorified through Jesus Christ. To him belong glory and dominion forever and ever. Amen. (1 Peter 4:10-11)

When I was 9 years old, my father took me on vacation to England. Before I left, Mother gave me some money to spend. I used this money at Harrods in London to buy a blue enamel bracelet, which I gave as a gift to Mother. She wore that bracelet for 40 years, more than any of her other jewelry. She had ultimately paid for the gift, but this in no way lessened her appreciation of its significance.

God is glorified as we use the gifts He gave us in service to His people.

So it is in our service to God. God is glorified as we use the gifts He gave us in service to His people.

As we assess our priorities and set our goals, it is good to glorify God through the gifts He has given us. God's people have real needs. God, in His grace, has equipped the members of His church to bless one another through the gifts He supplies.

Godly Worship

Worship, by definition, is ascribing worth to someone or something. What we value is what we worship. For this reason, as Paul noted, covetousness is idolatry (Colossians 3:5). When doing what we want becomes more valuable than doing what God wants, we have embraced will-worship (2:23). Authentic worship recounts the glory of God.

"Ascribe to the LORD the glory due his name," Psalm 29:2 instructs, "worship the LORD in the splendor of holiness." The excellence of worship is not in the entertainment of spectacle and pageantry. God is glorified when His holiness is reflected in the holiness of His people. By this standard, many of the productions conducted in congregations on Sunday mornings are not worship in any biblical sense. Embracing entertainment, they have abandoned the splendor of holiness.

As we assess our priorities and as we set our goals, it is good to glorify God through godly worship. Keeping the distinction between God-centered and man-centered worship is critical because our intent is glorifying God and bringing ourselves and those we lead into alignment with His will. In worship, appropriately leading God's people requires following God's direction. Going off in a direction of our own is not improvement; it is folly.

Choose God's Path

Day by day we are presented with a series of choices; it is as if we wind down a path in a dense forest. At regular intervals, we come to points of divergence. Do we go left, or do we go right? The trail chosen quickly turns, and we move on to the next point of decision. Every one of us is guided down life's path by the things we treasure. "For where your treasure is, there will your heart be also" (Luke 12:34).

The Bible says a great deal about the way the inner life of our desires propels us in one way or another. "Do you not know that if you present yourselves to anyone as obedient slaves, you are slaves of the one whom you obey, either of sin, which leads to death, or of obedience, which leads to righteousness?" (Romans 6:16).

> *The choices we make in life ultimately boil down to either seeking God's glory or seeking our personal gratification.*

Likewise, James 1:14 warns, "But each person is tempted when he is lured and enticed by his own desire." In contrast, the Savior promised in John 7:17, "If anyone's will is to do God's will, he will know whether the teaching is from God or whether I am speaking on my own authority." The choices we make in life ultimately boil down to either seeking God's glory or seeking our personal gratification.

The Israelites, delivered from the bondage of Egypt, were led by the glory of God through the wilderness. However, while Moses was on Mount Sinai, God's people lost their faith: "They made a golden calf in Horeb and worshiped a metal image. They exchanged the glory of God for the image of an ox that eats grass" (Psalm 106:19-20; Exodus 32:1-4).

We see this same story play out repeatedly as people choose a personal path rather than to be led by the glory of God. As Paul described it, "Claiming to be wise, they became fools, and exchanged the glory of the immortal God for images resembling mortal man and birds and animals and creeping things" (Romans 1:22-23).

Throughout life, we stand at the same crossroads, either we will follow the guidance given by the glory of God, or we will go down a path of humanism and materialism – worshiping "the creature rather than the Creator" (Romans 1:25).

Faith in God Guides Our Future

Management books are full of advice on how to set productive goals. Often the mechanics of goals are reduced to the acronym S.M.A.R.T. (specific, measurable, attainable, relevant and timed). This line of thought is designed to produce well-defined goals, monitored and regulated in their execution.

The best advice management theorists have put forward is to keep goals in alignment with your mission, which grows out of your vision. For Christians, our vision is faith in God's leadership, and our mission is to do His will.

Such faith, which gives glory to God, provides a path for every spiritual blessing, as we see in the example of Abraham: "No un-belief made him waver concerning the promise of God, but he grew strong in his faith as he gave glory to God, fully convinced that God was able to do what he had promised" (Romans 4:20-21).

The faith of Abraham guided him in each decision as he moved toward the goal set before him by God (Hebrews 11:8-10). As we set objectives for ourselves and for those we lead, we must look with faith if we want to see God's glory.

John 11 tells of the death of Lazarus, the brother of Mary and Martha. When Jesus arrived, He joined in the grieving and wept (v. 35). When He called for the tomb to be opened, Martha, fearing the odor of decomposition, objected. "Jesus said to her, 'Did I not tell you that if you believed you would see the glory of God?' " (vv. 39-40).

We must also believe if we want to see the glory of God, guided by the promise of Ephesians 3:20-21: "Now to him who is able to do far more abundantly than all that we ask or think, according to the power at work within us, to him be glory in the church and in Christ Jesus throughout all generations, forever and ever. Amen."

As we assess our priorities and as we set our goals, it is good to let faith in God guide us into His glorious future. Being men and women of faith will bring us and those we lead into greater alignment with the will of God. "Without faith it is impossible to please him," Hebrews 11:6 reminds us, "for whoever would draw near to God must believe that he exists and that he rewards those who seek him."

For REFLECTION

1. *How does recognizing God as the Creator provide a framework for setting goals?*

2. *What goals can we set for ourselves and/or with others relating to evangelism and Christian service?*

3. *What goals can we set for ourselves and/or with others relating to worship?*

4. *How can we keep ourselves accountable in pursuing our goals?*

NOTES: _____

_____

_____

_____

_____

_____

_____

_____

_____

_____

_____

_____

_____

_____

_____

_____

_____

_____

_____

5

Effective
STEWARDSHIP

Elisha, the prophet of God, was a problem for the king of Syria. When Syria campaigned against Israel, God informed Elisha concerning the attack. The prophet, in due course, would warn the king of Israel and thwart the assault. Finally, the king of Syria determined to eliminate Elisha so he could gain a clear path to attack Israel.

Sending a great army of horses and chariots by night, the king of Syria encircled the city where Elisha was staying. In the morning, Elisha's servant looked out and saw the Syrian army. In despair, he reported to the prophet, who helped his servant gain a clearer perspective: "Then Elisha prayed and said, 'O LORD, please open his eyes that he may see.' So the LORD opened the eyes of the young man, and he saw, and behold, the mountain was full of horses and chariots of fire all around Elisha" (2 Kings 6:17).

Elisha's servant needed to realize God had provided resources beyond what was apparent at first glance. When the servant looked from the standpoint of scarcity and need, he was overwhelmed. But a perspective of faith, based on divine revelation, provided a confident assurance of God's provision.

Open Your Eyes

"Open our eyes," we should constantly pray, ready to use the immeasurable blessings God has placed at our disposal. In every context, we can look either with eyes closed in fear or with eyes opened through faith.

Effective Christians have faith in God's promises of provision. They remember the words of James 1:17: "Every good gift and every perfect gift is from above, coming down from the Father of lights with whom there is no variation or shadow due to change." Giving in abundance is part of God's unchanging nature. God's grace shows itself in Him giving to us "all things" (Romans 8:32). He gave His Son. Why would God hold back on anything we need?

We can look either with eyes closed in fear or with eyes opened through faith.

We fail to excel in the Lord's work when, lacking faith, we disregard what God has given us. The parable of the talents shows that God provides all we need to be productive in His service (Matthew 25:14-30). Nestled in this parable is an important concept for Christian effectiveness: "For to everyone who has will more be given, and he will have an abundance. But from the one who has not, even what he has will be taken away" (v. 29).

Abundance is provided to the ones who have, while the ones who have not will be deprived. What then separates the ones who have from the ones who have not? Faith. As Jesus said in Mark 9:23, "All things are possible for one who believes."

A lack of faith is at the root of every failure chronicled in Scripture. The Israelites who failed to enter the Promised Land died in the wilderness because of their lack of faith. They did not believe the promises of God. In their disbelief, they did not receive God's blessings.

In contrast, the Bible continually promises achievement for those who trust in God's provision. As 2 Peter 1:3-4 reminds us,

> His divine power has granted to us all things that pertain to life and godliness, through the knowledge of him who called us to his own glory and excellence, by which he has granted to us his precious and very great promises, so that through them you may become partakers of the divine nature, having escaped from the corruption that is in the world because of sinful desire.

A mindset of scarcity, fear and deprivation will always look at the reasons for failure, while a mindset of abundance, faith and blessing will find a way to succeed.

Living Amid Unimaginable Riches

In the 1970s Batsell Barrett Baxter recorded a presentation of "Acres of Diamonds," a speech originally given by Russell H. Conwell at the end of 19th century. As a young man, this recording made a profound impact on me.

"Acres of Diamonds" begins with a story about a man who wanted to find diamonds so desperately that he sold his property and went off in search for them. Meanwhile, the new owner of his home discovered a rich diamond mine on the property. Conwell used this story to introduce examples of achievement, brilliance and service involving ordinary people who did extraordinary things using only the resources they had at hand. The message presented a gripping truth: Dig in your own backyard!

God has promised to "do far more abundantly than all that we ask or think, according to the power at work within us" (Ephesians 3:20). As Christians, we live amid unimaginable abundance – more precious than diamonds. Unless our eyes are opened that we may see, this abundance lies unappreciated and unused.

In the early days of colonization, Portuguese ships bound for Brazil often ran short of water as they crossed the Atlantic. Dehydration leading to an agonizing death was the end of many sailors. Sadly, these deaths were often unnecessary. Each second the massive Amazon River pours almost 60 million gallons of water into the Atlantic Ocean. This massive influx of fresh water actually dilutes salt in the ocean for up to 100 miles offshore. Long before they were in sight of land, the sailors were surrounded by more fresh water than they could ever use.

In the same way God's blessings engulf us, providing all we need, but we often are blind to the Lord's abundant provisions.

Often, ordinary things that surround our everyday lives have the potential to provide extraordinary blessings. We frequently say that bacteriologist Sir Alexander Fleming "discovered" penicillin in 1928. *Penicillium notatum,* however, is a common mold that has been around since creation. Fleming was studying a disease-causing bacteria. When his lab assistant left a window open overnight, mold spores covered the bacteria.

At first, Fleming was very irritated at the contamination, but as he was about to throw the bacteria away, he saw something interesting. He noticed that the mold had prevented the bacteria from making new cell walls and reproducing. Although the mold was nothing new – for centuries people had thrown out food contaminated by this blue-green fungus – Fleming discovered the use of the mold in fighting infection.

We should develop a mindset of endless possibility, realizing God may give seemingly insignificant things phenomenal importance. "Open our eyes that we may see," should be the prayer of every Christian. The gifts of God are "irrevocable" (Romans 11:29). Nothing happens by chance. Inventorying each aspect of our lives, we should look for evidence of grace.

Early in the 20th century, American psychiatrist Karl A. Menninger noted, "Attitudes are more important than facts." This echoed an earlier observation of American philosopher and psychologist William James: "The greatest discovery of my generation is that a human being can alter his life by altering his attitudes of mind."

This emphasis on perspective is in keeping with the first habit identified by Stephen R. Covey in his book *The 7 Habits of Highly Effective People.* Be proactive. Covey highlights the primary meaning of the term "proactive," as coined by Viktor E. Frankl, as the principle of personal choice.

A person can either be proactive or reactive when it comes to how he responds to life. When a person is reactive, he points a finger at other people and circumstances, blaming them for his problems. In contrast, a proactive person takes responsibility for every aspect of his life. Initiative and taking action then follows.

Covey also argues that people are different from animals in that they have self-consciousness. They have the ability to detach themselves and observe themselves and to think about their thoughts. This attribute gives mankind the power not to be affected by circumstances. Free will lets us choose the attitude with which we face life.

We need to choose an attitude of abundance rather than an attitude of scarcity. We need to see that our glass is never only half-full – it is always completely filled with what we need (for air is more essential even than water). We need to value what we have rather than focus on what we do not have, for this is the heart of the 10th commandment: "You shall not covet" (Exodus 20:17).

Living a life of contentment comes from the gratitude of faith. Without an outlook informed by faith, there can be no abundance of life – even in the midst of an abundance of possessions.

The Gift of God's Grace

"The kingdom of heaven is like treasure hidden in a field," Jesus told us in Matthew 13:44, "which a man found and covered up. Then in his joy he goes and sells all that he has and buys that field." One of the treasures hidden in our lives is God's enabling grace. So where do we find this gift that God has in mind for us to enjoy?

Finding God's Grace in Personal Identity

The phrase "know thyself," a phrase pivotal to the teachings of Greek philosophers, was inscribed on the ancient temple of Apollo at Delphi. Believing in the gracious provision of God in our lives, what do we have that contains the resources of God's grace? Often we permit ourselves to forget the many and abundant blessings of God woven into the very fabric of our lives.

Every member of the church has natural ability given by God. In her book *Gifts Differing*, Isabel Briggs Myers catalogs the way people differ by the way they deal with the world, process information and communicate with others. While written from the standpoint of secular research, Myers gives a nod to the source of these different abilities. In the dedication for her book, she quotes Romans 12:4-8 (KJV): "For as we have many members in one body, and all members have not the same office: So we, being many, are one body in Christ, and every one members one of another. Having then gifts differing … " (vv. 4-6). As Christians, we know that every gift is from God and is to be used to His glory.

> *Without an outlook informed by faith, there can be no abundance of life – even in the midst of an abundance of possessions.*

Each person possesses attributes opening doors of effective service to God. These mental, physical and social qualities confer benefits on each individual. Effective Christians know their natural strengths and build on them, humbly recognizing that all the things that make them uniquely gifted are blessings from God.

In 1 Corinthians 4:7 Paul wrote: "For who sees anything different in you? What do you have that you did not receive? If then you received it, why do you boast as if you did not receive it?" Recognizing God as the source of our abilities, we should use them in the Lord's service.

Finding God's Grace in Experience

Everything we let into our lives shapes us in one way or another. Cicero, in his ancient study of oratory, spoke of the incidental influence of the books we read: "When I walk in the sun, though I may walk for another purpose, yet it naturally happens that I gain a deeper color; so, when I have read ... books ... , I can perceive that my language acquires a complexion ... from my intercourse with them."

> *Everything we let into our lives shapes us in one way or another.*

Each thing that touches us leaves an impression. In good and wholesome influences, God is providing us with an ever-expanding treasury of resources to use in His service. As no one has our exact storehouse of experiences to draw from, we are uniquely gifted to serve God through our lives.

As with natural abilities, the resources gained from experience may go unnoticed because, like the air we breathe, they are everywhere. Sometimes we need to take a step back and inventory the ebb and flow of our lives, recognizing "it is God who works in you, both to will and to work for his good pleasure" (Philippians 2:13). A hidden treasure of experience in the field of your life may be waiting to be uncovered and used in the Lord's service.

Finding God's Grace in Material Abundance

Without dwelling on the subject at length, for we live in a materialistic age, our physical possessions offer opportunities that are graciously given. John Wesley's familiar admonition well expresses the biblical ideal: "Earn all you can, give all you can, save all you can."

Even the poorest person living in the developed world has resources that would seem overwhelming in most other places and times. How we use our material wealth is often a strong indicator of the priorities we place in life. In 1 Timothy 6:17-19, we read Paul's instruction concerning the stewardship of material abundance:

> As for the rich in this present age, charge them not to be haughty, nor to set their hopes on the uncertainty of riches, but on God, who richly provides us with everything to enjoy. They are to do good, to be rich in good works, to be generous and ready to share, thus storing up treasure for themselves as a good foundation for the future, so that they may take hold of that which is truly life.

Beyond direct monetary gifts, our material abundance has given us opportunities for hospitality and service in a wide range of situations. While we must never focus exclusively on the use of money, the Bible makes it clear we are responsible before God for how we use the wealth He places at our disposal. Wealth is a gift from God, and we must answer for how we use it.

Finding God's Grace in Others

"No man is an island," English poet John Donne rightly observed. When considering our association with others, we immediately think of our connectedness with family.

The Bible encourages this outlook of family as a transgenerational treasury of blessing. Looking back, we see how a righteous man is a blessing to his children and grandchildren (Proverbs 20:7). We see Timothy being trained in the Scripture by his mother and grandmother (2 Timothy 1:5). Looking forward, we see how children and grandchildren are referred to in the Bible as blessings from God (Psalms 127:3). Our families are a great resource that God has provided in our lives.

Through association with godly friends, we become more effective in the Lord's service.

As with all blessings, God gives us families as a means of effective service in His work. There should be a stewardship of relationships even as there is a stewardship of material possessions, for the people God has placed in our lives are more precious than financial wealth.

Like family, friendship provides an opportunity to experience the gracious gifts of God. "Iron sharpens iron, and one man sharpens another" (Proverbs 27:17). Through association with godly friends, we become more effective in the Lord's service.

When faced with a challenge, the Bible encourages us to turn to our friends. "A friend loves at all times, and a brother is born for adversity" (Proverbs 17:17).

Beyond friends and family, there are many associates and even strangers who are willing to help if asked. Many experts in various fields are delighted to share their expertise. This power of asking is amplified where there is a social connection, such as in alumni groups, civic organizations, service clubs and (especially) the church.

There are "acres of diamonds" we can gather, hidden in the field of the vast social web that binds us all together. With all people, we must be open to the contribution others can make in our lives, but we must be careful never to let them lead us astray. As Paul commanded, "Test everything; hold fast what is good" (1 Thessalonians 5:21).

Finding God's Grace in the Entire World

God causes the rain to fall "on the just and on the unjust" (Matthew 5:45). While Christians have many blessings and opportunities that are unique to their lives, there is what theologians call "common grace": that is, God's gifts that are open to the broad scope of mankind.

All we possess belongs to God. We are accountable to Him for how we use the blessings He has given us.

We look at nature and see in its beauty and in the wisdom of its order a great spiritual resource, which (being universal) we often take for granted. "Consider the lilies of the field, how they grow" Jesus reminded us (Matthew 6:28).

Within the framework of Western culture, there are blessings of a free and open society, a democratic tradition, and a rich cultural history that is broadly available to all.

"If I have seen further it is by standing on the shoulders of giants," English physicist Sir Isaac Newton observed. This intellectual heritage is a vast resource God has placed at our disposal. The great books of Western culture, such as the compilation collected by Mortimer Adler, are available in every major library. The stewardship of the mind is a vital concern for effective Christians.

Also broadly available are the spiritual blessings of the Christian faith. Open to all, although accessed by few, are the blessings of salvation. Revelation 22:17 shows the universal invitation: "The Spirit and the Bride say, 'Come.' And let the one who hears say, 'Come.' And let the one who is thirsty come; let the one who desires take the water of life without price."

Turning to God provides vast resources enriching every area of life. Whoever desires can freely drink of this "water of life." Astute Christians will find the treasure of God's blessing hidden in the field of the Lord's church.

The Word of God is widely available – if not widely read. But for those who do read the Bible, they find a resource of spiritual power and a resource for competency in "every good work" (2 Timothy 3:17).

Those who accept the gospel will also find in worship – singing, communion, prayer, contribution and instruction – and in fellowship great resources that are available to all who belong to Christ. In all of these, and in many other ways, God is equipping His people through His church.

Using Resources:
The Stewardship Imperative

"Having gifts," Romans 12:6 enjoins, "use them." Burying our resources in the ground or hiding them under a basket are not options (Matthew 25:25; 5:15). As we have opportunity, we are to do good (Galatians 6:10). Identifying the gifts of God obligates us to use them. We cannot pass by on the "other side" (Luke 10:30-37).

This principle of stewardship recognizes that all we possess, in the broadest sense, belongs to God. We are accountable to Him for how we use the blessings He has given us. Ultimately, a correct understanding of resources must come from a mind trained to look through the eyes of faith.

Isaiah prayed, "O Lord, you will ordain peace for us, for you have indeed done for us all our works" (Isaiah 26:12). As we grow to recognize the work of God in every area of our lives, we will grow adept at identifying the resources He has placed in our lives for our use in His service.

For
REFLECTION

1. *What resources could be better used in your family or congregation?*

2. *Why do people dwell so much on the negative that they overlook the positive things in life?*

3. *What can we do to cultivate a spirit of thanksgiving in our lives?*

4. *How can we help other people look beyond their limitations and see the blessings God has placed in their lives?*

NOTES: _____

_____

_____

_____

_____

_____

_____

_____

_____

_____

_____

_____

_____

_____

_____

_____

6

Effective
PLANNING

"The sum of your word is truth," Psalm 119:160 reminds us, "and every one of your righteous rules endures forever." When looking at any point of doctrine, care must be taken to consider all the Bible says. Many times error comes in when we leave some of what God has said out of the equation. Truth only emerges from the combined whole of what God tells us in His Word.

A Balanced Approach

The need for holistic understanding shows through in our approach to planning. Some passages of Scripture, in isolation, make it sound evil and arrogant to plan. Consider, for example, the words of Christ in Matthew 6:25-34:

> Therefore I tell you, do not be anxious about your life, what you will eat or what you will drink, nor about your body, what you will put on. Is not life more than food, and the body more than clothing? Look at the birds of the air: they neither sow nor reap nor gather into barns, and yet your heavenly Father feeds them. Are you not of more value than they? And which of you by being anxious can add a single hour to his span of life? And

why are you anxious about clothing? Consider the lilies of the field, how they grow: they neither toil nor spin, yet I tell you, even Solomon in all his glory was not arrayed like one of these. But if God so clothes the grass of the field, which today is alive and tomorrow is thrown into the oven, will he not much more clothe you, O you of little faith? Therefore do not be anxious, saying, "What shall we eat?" or "What shall we drink?" or "What shall we wear?" For the Gentiles seek after all these things, and your heavenly Father knows that you need them all. But seek first the kingdom of God and his righteousness, and all these things will be added to you. Therefore do not be anxious about tomorrow, for tomorrow will be anxious for itself. Sufficient for the day is its own trouble.

Taken alone, this admonition seems to discourage planning. Jesus, however, also said:

For which of you, desiring to build a tower, does not first sit down and count the cost, whether he has enough to complete it? Otherwise, when he has laid a foundation and is not able to finish, all who see it begin to mock him, saying, "This man began to build and was not able to finish." (Luke 14:28-30)

By itself, this warning elevates planning to the status of an imperative. Failing to plan, we compromise our effectiveness and fall into foolish ruin. However, God's truth is neither found in obsessive and arrogant planning nor in an irresponsible disregard for the future. God's truth shines through in Scripture's encouragement of humble stewardship.

Recognizing God's ultimate role in guiding our lives, we are still responsible for taking action.

James 4:13-17 presents this balanced approach – that of maintaining humility while planning for the future:

Come now, you who say, "Today or tomorrow we will go into such and such a town and spend a year there and trade and make a profit" – yet you do not know what tomorrow will bring. What is your life? For you are a mist that appears for a little time and then vanishes. Instead you ought to say, "If the Lord wills, we will live and do this or that." As it is, you boast in your arrogance. All such boasting is evil. So whoever knows the right thing to do and fails to do it, for him it is sin.

Recognizing God's ultimate role in guiding our lives, we are still responsible for taking action. Avoiding both arrogance and apathy, James encouraged us to decisive action tempered by humility. This same outlook is found in the quote attributed to 16th-century Spanish priest Ignatius Loyola: "Pray as if everything depends on God, and work as if everything depends on you."

Prayer and Planning

Prayer and planning properly consider two realities: the mind of God and the mind of the Christian. The spiritual reality of prayer realizes there is a God who hears. One of my favorite lines from *Les Misérables* is "What's the use of praying if there's nobody who hears?" The despair of that thought turns into joy when we realize there is someone who hears. Prayer to God is more than mere meditation. God hears, cares and answers prayer.

In prayer, we must never fall into the shallow "name it and claim it" heresy. God is not a genie in a lamp mindlessly granting wishes. He is Lord. His thoughts are higher than our thoughts; His ways are higher than our ways (Isaiah 55:8-9). God is so great that He does not need our insight to inform Him of what He should do, although He loves us and asks for our prayers.

God is so great that He is never surprised by our prayers so as to be reduced to a last minute miracle in order to save a situation spiraling out of control. Do not think of your last minute prayers catching God by surprise. In Isaiah, the Lord said: "Before they call, I will answer; while they are yet speaking I will hear" (65:24). That

Prayer is the ultimate reality check.

our prayers matter in the workings of God is a great mystery; we cannot explain how this is true. But we know it is because God has told us so.

While prayer to God is more than mere meditation, the spiritual reality of prayer also has an effect within us. We believe we are speaking to God when we pray. This reality produces several adjustments in our thinking. First, approaching God in prayer is appropriately humbling. As Jesus prayed, "Nevertheless, not as I will, but as you will" (Matthew 26:39). Approaching God in prayer is also refining. Remembering who we are and who we are addressing – One who is holy and all-knowing – helps us cut through any pretense hiding impure motives.

The famous quote attributed to President Abraham Lincoln about fooling "some of the people all of the time" was intended to promote honesty. Yet our chances of fooling any given person at any point in time is very good. We can and do deceive other people, even as we deceive ourselves. But we cannot deceive God. When this is properly understood, prayer becomes the ultimate reality check.

We should constantly ask how our tentative plans fit into God's eternal plan.

Prayer can also help build into a written plan. Sometimes we act as if spontaneity in prayer is more spiritual than deliberation. However, many of the greatest prayers recorded in Scripture bear the marks of careful composition. This care is appropriate as we plan to approach the Lord. Not only were prayers carefully composed, they were deliberately preserved as a means of using the truths they contained. One of the advantages of maintaining a written record of the prayers we offer to God is that we can monitor and maintain the direction of our thinking on any subject.

Developing written plans is one of the greatest practices we can embrace for building greater effectiveness. Careful review of how these plans were executed and documentation of lessons learned aid in future application.

Planning and Enhanced Effectiveness

As we develop the practice of planning and a prayerful outlook, we will not only find ourselves more effective in our service to the Lord, but also find new opportunities for service. There is a biblical principle of momentum, either for better or for worse. We see this in the parable of the talents, recorded in Matthew 25.

In this parable, a man gave three servants charge over various sums of money. The two who were productive were rewarded with greater responsibility, while the one who was unproductive was punished: "So take the talent from him and give it to him who has the ten talents. For to everyone who has will more be given, and he will have an abundance. But from the one who has not, even what he has will be taken away" (Matthew 25:28-29).

Often in the midst of productive service in the church, doors will open providing opportunities for even more service. But in all of this, God must be a real presence in our lives every step of the way. "Commit your work to the LORD," Proverbs 16:3 says, "and your plans will be established."

One way to make sure your plans are committed to the Lord is to maintain a commitment to His Word. In Scripture we have God's perfect plan for His people. We should constantly ask how our tentative plans fit into His eternal plan. We should always seek to do the Lord's work in the Lord's way – to obey His commands and to learn from the examples He has given us in Scripture.

Another way to make sure our plans are committed to the Lord is to maintain a commitment to His church. "Without counsel plans fail," Proverbs 15:22 says, "but with many advisers they succeed." Humbling ourselves before God, we should have the humility to seek the help of His people in doing His work.

One of the great dangers undermining Christian effectiveness is the arrogance to imagine we can do everything ourselves without assistance. Seeking wise counsel from God's people will help us plan effectively to abound in the work of the Lord.

For
REFLECTION

1. *What are the dangers of failing to plan?*

2. *Why should Christians keep a level of tentativeness in their planning?*

3. *How can prayer lead to more effective planning?*

4. *How does Bible study help us develop our plans?*

NOTES: _____

_____

_____

_____

_____

_____

_____

_____

_____

_____

_____

_____

_____

_____

_____

_____

_____

_____

_____

_____

7

Effective STANDARDS

"How faithful does the church have to be, anyway?" I have enjoyed asking my more progressive friends this question. As they begin explaining why a rigorous approach in religion is unimportant, I shift the question and ask, "Then how faithful does your spouse have to be?" Jaws drop; eyebrows go up.

As important as faithfulness is in marriage, our fidelity to Jesus Christ is even more important. Christians must work to maintain standards in every area of life, for in all things "you are serving the Lord Christ" (Colossians 3:24).

Why Maintaining Standards Is Difficult

Of all the tasks of effective Christian service, maintaining standards is the most thankless, yet "it is required of stewards that they be found faithful" (1 Corinthians 4:2). Fidelity is not measured by how we do the easy things, but in how we do the things we would rather avoid. Maintaining standards is a hard and thankless work for several reasons.

People Want the New and Trendy

Maintaining standards is a conservative rather than a creative endeavor. It seeks the preservation of a set order rather than experimentation with the new. A Christian who is adept at maintaining standards will often go unappreciated. If nothing has changed, no one will notice.

More than that, when a change agent attempts to impose an innovation upon us, popular sentiment (especially among the immature and unstable) will flow toward the new and against the old.

In the days of Jeremiah, we read of the popularity of innovative religion. But Jeremiah 5:31 closes with this pointed question: "The prophets prophesy falsely, and the priests rule at their direction; my people love to have it so, but what will you do when the end comes?"

We want choice. We go to the ice cream shop and expect dozens of flavors. In religion, this same expectation exists. We want a contemporary service to compete with traditional worship. Our "youth culture" has led us into a shallow selfishness in the church – a selfishness that calls for a continual parade of new things. Maintaining standards will often put Christians at odds with the spirit of our age.

People Want Only the Good News

Again from the prophet Jeremiah, we see the appeal of false religion that promises salvation without repentance: "They have healed the wound of my people lightly, saying, 'Peace, Peace,' when there is no peace" (Jeremiah 6:14).

Maintaining standards is hard because it deals with hard realities. More popular is today's approach of "easy believism." This is Christianity "lite" – all of the blessings and none of the commitment.

Years ago, when I was a student at Lipscomb University, most of my classmates were members of the church of Christ, but one young man I befriended came from a completely non-religious background.

Lipscomb required daily Bible classes, and my non-Christian friend chose an advanced course titled "Systematic Christian Doctrine" with Harvey Floyd as his first Bible class. Halfway through the term after being presented with the gospel, this young man was baptized into Christ. However, we learned that the new convert was sharing an apartment with his live-in girlfriend.

Floyd and Batsell Barrett Baxter, the Bible department chairman, studied with the student and "explained to him the way of God more accurately" (Acts 18:26). In time, this new Christian explained to his girlfriend that because she would not marry him, they could not continue to live together.

Floyd and Baxter were Christian gentlemen in every sense. They practiced courtesy and kindness in addressing this situation. As committed

Christians, they addressed the hard truths the student needed to hear – not merely offering platitudes he might have wanted to hear.

People Are Tempted to Shoot the Messenger

Many preachers have lost their jobs because speaking the truth was not politically expedient. "Which of the prophets did your fathers not persecute?" asked Stephen. As if to prove his point, the Jews proceeded to kill Stephen (Acts 7:52ff).

We are seeing our culture "shoot the messenger" in the many ways the message of repentance is being labeled as "hate speech." In Europe, many examples exist of religious people being silenced by secular governments when they have spoken against homosexuality. Closer to home, Canadian churches opposed to homosexuality are having their rights eliminated.

Christians need to maintain their standards in the face of persecution.

Even in the U.S., the Supreme Court used the "international human rights law" as the basis of overturning the sodomy laws in Texas (Lawrence v. Texas, 2003). How long will it be before the same logic leads to European-style religious oppression in America?

Being forewarned is being forearmed. Every congregation should prepare Christians to maintain their standards in the face of persecution. However, how can we resist the pressure to compromise with the world when we are unwilling to stand against worldly trends within the church? As Walter Kelly's "Pogo" cartoon in 1970 stated, "We have met the enemy and he is us."

The Trojan Horse of Compromise

The New Testament contains far more warnings about sabotage from the inside than assault from the outside. But there are assurances that when outside persecutions come, we will be fine. "Do not fear those who kill the body," Jesus told us (Matthew 10:28). Even if we lose our lives, we are not lost – as long as we are faithful. The real loss of eternal life comes not from oppression on the outside but from corruption on the inside.

Compromise has threatened the Lord's work from the beginning, as Paul warned Timothy: "For the time is coming when people will not endure sound teaching, but having itching ears they will accumulate for themselves teachers to suit their own passions" (2 Timothy 4:3).

Compromise is a dangerous thing. Many years ago, I asked an older preacher how pointed he would be in preaching against specific sins. His answer still leaves me cold: "As much as the traffic will bear." This approach, which is far too common, continually lowers our standards. Like a perverse game of spiritual limbo, we keep going lower and lower.

Would we sell our soul for a million dollars? If not, would we sell our soul for the approval of other people? At least Esau got a bowl of soup for his birthright. Often we sell out at a much lower price.

We want an acquaintance to be our friend, but we know his lifestyle is immoral. Do we hide the light of God's morality rather than letting it shine (Luke 11:33-36)? When we are perpetually silent concerning the teaching of Scripture, we are in complicity with the error of the world. Paul told the Ephesian elders, "I am innocent of the blood of all, for I did not shrink from declaring to you the whole counsel of God" (Acts 20:26-27). Applying this same standard to our lives, do we have blood on our hands?

> *When we are perpetually silent concerning the teaching of Scripture, we are in complicity with the error of the world.*

Much of our lack of focus in the church comes from a lack of appreciation for the reality of eternal punishment that awaits those who are not right with God. As members of the church we often act as if we do not really believe in hell.

James 5:20 reminds us, "Let him know that whoever brings back a sinner from his wandering will save his soul from death and will cover a multitude of sins." The difference between faithfulness and apostasy is the difference between spending eternity with God in heaven and spending eternity separated from God in hell.

The reality of eternal punishment is a powerful motivator for Christian service. Knowing the loving grace of God toward sinners, we should press forward to make sure more people are blessed in the obedience of faith. The coming judgment is motivation for evangelism and vigilance. We should have an equal passion both to see people come to the Lord and to stay with the Lord ourselves.

A Foundation for Spiritual Excellence

Visiting the home of Alexander Campbell in Bethany, W.Va., I learned that the Disciples of Christ, who maintain the site, have installed a "prayer labyrinth" beside his home for the purpose of spiritual growth. Campbell would have been appalled at this bit of medieval Catholic mysticism befouling his grounds. In contrast, Campbell sought a closer communion with God through a careful study of the Bible and a diligent application of its teachings.

Diminishing the role of Scripture, progressives among churches of Christ, as well as those among the denominations, seek spiritual experiences in weird, wacky and esoteric practices. These have the empty allure of fool's gold.

In our quest for new spiritual adventures, we sometimes forget the greatest adventure is each day taking up a cross and following Jesus (Luke 9:23). As in the lyrics of the hymn "Trust and Obey," "When we walk with the Lord / In the light of His Word, / What a glory He sheds on our way." The glory of the Lord and the privilege of walking with Him are only found in the light of His Word. The truth of Scripture provides the standard that will bless every aspect of our lives.

Jesus commended the church in Philadelphia, noting their devotion to the truth of Scripture and praising their consistency in maintaining the good confession. "I know your works," Jesus said in Revelation 3:8. "Behold, I have set before you an open door, which no one is able to shut. I know that you have but little power, and yet you have kept my word and have not denied my name." Rewarding their faithfulness, Jesus gave them "an open door."

In literature, the image of an open door is used metaphorically to represent an opportunity, and Scripture makes use of this image in many passages (cf. Acts 14:27; 1 Corinthians 16:9; 2 Corinthians 2:12; Colossians 4:3).

The church in Philadelphia demonstrated faith in the word of the Lord and faithfulness in the conduct of their lives. What was the reward for their faithful service? Jesus gave them opportunity for more service. He gave them an open door. This example illustrates the point Jesus often made that the one who has will be given more (Luke 19:26, Mark 4:25).

The more we serve the Lord, the more opportunities for service we will find. But remember, an open door is an invitation to service. It is a starting point rather than the finish line.

What open doors has God called us to step through? A kaleidoscopic range of possibilities comes in and out of our lives, opening a wide variety of exciting opportunities. The single key that opens all of these doors is faithfulness to Jesus Christ.

For
REFLECTION

1. *Why do Christians sometimes avoid maintaining standards?*

2. *How does the pattern of faith found in the New Testament provide a standard for the church in our age?*

3. *How can the church be more diligent in maintaining the standards God has given?*

4. *How can we avoid "cherry-picking" the aspects of Christianity we find attractive in contrast to the ones we find difficult?*

NOTES: _____

_____

_____

_____

_____

_____

_____

_____

_____

_____

_____

_____

_____

_____

8

Effective
FELLOWSHIP

A mob pushes its way through the streets of Paris. A man follows after the mob, saying: "There go the people. I must follow them, for I am their leader." Alexandre Ledru-Rollin's joke describing political instability in 19th-century France highlights a vital principle: Leadership is relational – a person cannot be a leader in isolation. While he or she may lead only one other person, leadership normally occurs in a group.

Effective Christians know the needs of their group, which may not be the same as the needs of any one person in the group. Maintaining a church building, for example, does not just benefit one particular church member but provides the whole congregation with a place to meet. A balance must be maintained to understand the needs of the group and the needs of each member. For this reason, a central question for effective Christian service is how members of the group relate to one another and how they relate to the group as a whole.

Understanding Different Groups

Most of us belong to many groups that are essentially impersonal. I subscribe to an online edition of the Nashville, Tenn., daily newspaper,

The Tennessean. This makes me part of a group of subscribers numbering in the thousands, but I have no further connection to the members of the group. I do not even know another group member's name. The leaders of this group relate to me in providing news and information, but there is no personal relationship between us.

Sadly, many people treat religion this way. They attend worship services as anonymous spectators. Others take isolation a step further, making faith a completely private matter. Without gathering with others at all, they seek edification through the media or through the inner light of contemplation. Certainly, God expects His church to have more cohesion than this selfish solitude.

In contrast to the many impersonal associations of our lives, we participate in other groups that are relational but still limited to a well-defined slice of our lives. Such groups exist as members interrelate but have little influence on one another's lives except as they gather for a particular purpose. These groups range in time-commitment and importance, but all such groups define something we do, not something we are.

The workplace is this sort of group. Most people hold several different positions in the course of a career, moving through several jobs. Essentially all people, except extreme workaholics, have private lives completely unrelated to their professional pursuits. In time, they usually retire and leave connections with co-workers in the past.

Participation in other groups proves even more transient. Many athletic centers field pick-up games of basketball – teams made up on the spot. There are no consequences beyond the final score in terms of standings or future commitment. The team relates together as a cohesive group but only for the duration of the game.

> *Being a Christian is more than something we do; it is who we are.*

Some Christians play a pick-up game of religion. Earnest and engaged for the moment, they have no lasting commitment. Other Christians, with more serious intent, view religion much as they do their profession. Conscientiously, they want to succeed and are willing to work toward that goal. However, for them religion is what one does during a portion of his or her life. This approach gives people an excuse to go "off the clock" in their Christianity and is responsible for many "retiring" from Christian service, even as they retire from secular employment.

Membership in the church, however, differs fundamentally from participation in entertainment or employment. Being a Christian is more than something we do some of the time. Being a Christian is who we are all of the time. Membership in the church is not like attending a concert, playing a sport, or working for a corporation. Rather, membership in the church is like having a nationality or even more – it is like being part of a family. It is who we are, not just what we do.

The Needs of the Church

Members of the church, as part of an eternal family, have an obligation to consider each individual member in a way we would not in other sorts of groups. In a corporation or on a sports team, for example, each member of the group is expendable for the good of the whole. In the church, however, the value of each soul is infinite. As the Savior reminds us:

> What do you think? If a man has a hundred sheep, and one of them has gone astray, does he not leave the ninety-nine on the mountains and go in search of the one that went astray? And if he finds it, truly, I say to you, he rejoices over it more than over the ninety-nine that never went astray. So it is not the will of my Father who is in heaven that one of these little ones should perish. (Matthew 18:12-14)

God's priority must be our priority in the church as well. There are no expendable members of the Lord's family.

The Importance of Listening

Appropriate communication is a humane act because each person is precious in the eyes of God. Inappropriate communication is an affront to humane values and, even more, an affront to God, who is creator of all people (cf. Malachi 2:10). There is human validation in listening and unchristianlike arrogance in not listening.

Although the emphasis on individuals requires listening to each person's concerns, Christians must avoid reacting to every complaint as if it were valid and to every suggestion as if it had merit. God warned both against the prating of fools and against the way of the scoffer (cf. Proverbs 23:3; 21:24). "Test everything," 1 Thessalonians 5:21 reminds us, "hold fast what is good."

The church must neither be bullied by a vocal minority nor deceived by conventional wisdom. Truth is not determined by majority vote. Opinions should be weighed not counted.

The Need for Understanding

Another important need of the church is for members to be understanding of one another. When someone takes a complaint to a leader, he must remember he likely does not have all of the information about the situation. Without being condescending, he must seek to understand the other side and avoid reacting too quickly.

A depth of understanding often develops with age. A young executive, so the story goes, asked his CEO the secret of his success.

"I make good decisions," the CEO replied.

"How can I learn to make good decisions?"

"You need experience."

"How do I get experience?"

"You make some bad decisions."

As church members practice communication, inevitably, they will misunderstand one another. But they can learn from these mistakes, refusing to waste the opportunity to build skills in greater understanding.

The Gospel Blimp

Joseph T. Bayly identified the danger of following a popular but wrongheaded trend in his humorous 1960 story *The Gospel Blimp*. This story tells the adventures of a group of well-intentioned but misguided believers who desire to reach their neighbors for Christ. Rather than relying on the biblical approaches of preaching, teaching and personal work, they devise the plan for the Gospel Blimp, a flying billboard spelling out the gospel, announcing its message through loudspeakers and blanketing the city with tracts that drop from the blimp's lofty heights.

Truth is not determined by majority vote.

The rest of the story tells the initiation and expansion of this ministry. Not surprisingly, an enterprise of this scale takes up vast amounts of time and resources, and because of its high profile, it requires significant public relations efforts. However, none of the time, effort or expenditures directly related to simply doing the Lord's work in the Lord's way was required.

In the end, one of the original founders of the ministry begins to see the truth. After the blimp ministry leaders decide to partner with secular organizations, diluting the message of the gospel with some non-gospel messages in return for increased donations to the blimp, he realizes the Gospel Blimp ministry has become primarily about the continuation of the ministry and not about doing the Lord's work.

This modern-day parable is a cutting reflection on many trends in the church. Christians should ask themselves from time to time if they are more concerned about the "blimp" or about the gospel. It is very easy to place importance on the trappings of ministry and to let the Lord's work go by the wayside. In assessing the needs of Christians and of congregations, we must never permit non-biblical concerns to overshadow the demands of Scripture.

> *We must never permit non-biblical concerns to overshadow the demands of Scripture.*

Godliness in Meeting Needs

There are many secular approaches to meeting needs. Socialism, for example, looks only at materialism and the redistribution of wealth in addressing human needs. Some secular humanists include an existential element in meeting needs (e.g., Abraham Maslow with his hierarchy of needs or Viktor E. Frankl in his quest for authenticity). However, all secular approaches fall short because of their failure in addressing the ultimate human need: the need to be prepared for what happens after we die and for the judgment.

The work of the church often gets off on the wrong foot because we permit secular assumptions to frame our thinking rather than permitting ourselves to be led by the Word of God. It really does not matter whether the ungodly game plan comes from psychology, marketing or entertainment. We cannot permit the devil to frame the questions and expect godliness in the answers. "For no good tree bears bad fruit," Jesus reminded us, "nor again does a bad tree bear good fruit" (Luke 6:43).

Solomon commented on a secular approach to meaning and values in the book of Ecclesiastes. He looked at wealth, education and power – all the things that secular humanists value. In contrast to any man-made approach, Solomon concluded with this simple admonition: "The end of the matter; all has been heard. Fear God and keep his commandments, for this is the whole duty of man. For God will bring every deed into judgment, with every secret thing, whether good or evil" (Ecclesiastes 12:13-14).

> *The greatest service we can give anyone is to lead them out of error and into the truth of the gospel.*

This same framework was put forward by the Savior when He reminded us:

> Therefore do not be anxious, saying, "What shall we eat?" or "What shall we drink?" or "What shall we wear?" For the Gentiles seek after all these things, and your heavenly Father knows that you need them all. But seek first the kingdom of God and his righteousness, and all these things will be added to you. (Matthew 6:31-33)

We should always seek to understand the needs of the group and of individuals from a divine perspective. In particular, leaders in the church should prayerfully consider the need for correction, encouragement and equipment.

The Need for Correction

A universal need of people (both individually and collectively) is the need for correction. The work of an evangelist is to "reprove, rebuke, and exhort" (2 Timothy 4:2). Elders are to convict the erring (Titus 1:9). The Son of God came to call sinners, not to congratulate the righteous (Luke 5:32).

The greatest service we can give anyone is to lead them out of error and into the truth of the gospel: "My brothers, if anyone among you wanders from the truth and someone brings him back, let him know that whoever brings back a sinner from his wandering will save his soul from death and will cover a multitude of sins" (James 5:19-20).

We must speak "the truth in love," as Paul instructed in Ephesians 4:15, but we must be sure we speak the truth. Absent from the truth, there is no real love.

However, speaking the truth is hard work. The easy way is to go along and get along, but the easy way leads to compromise and dissolution. Lanny Henninger, who served more than 20 years as the preacher for University Avenue Church of Christ in Austin, Texas, observed, "Following the course of least resistance makes for crooked rivers and crooked men." He was right. The greatest danger facing the church is compromise. We are in danger of selling out from within, not of being overwhelmed from without.

Further, we should remember the warning God gave to the prophet Ezekiel, which certainly applies to us as well: "If I say to the wicked, O wicked one, you shall surely die, and you do not speak to warn the wicked to turn from his way, that wicked person shall die in his iniquity, but his blood I will require at your hand" (Ezekiel 33:8).

If we compromise the truth in order to join the popular trend, we will be entering the broad way that leads to destruction (Matthew 7:13). The need for heartfelt repentance belongs to each Christian.

The Need for Encouragement

Although we must convict one another of the need to repent, repentance without grace leaves us in despair. We must encourage one another with the good news of Jesus Christ.

Each one of us falls short and needs forgiveness. Further, each one of us faces adversity, uncertainty and heartache. We need the encouragement that can only come from the gospel of Christ.

In His grace, God has provided assurance to us of His loving care. In baptism and in the Lord's Supper, Christians are blessed to see the love of God that comes to us in Christ. As we worship in prayer and in song, our hearts are revived in God's truth.

Of the many ways available to bring encouragement to God's people, one of the most powerful is to bring the Word of God: "For whatever was written in former days was written for our instruction, that through endurance and through the encouragement of the Scriptures we might have hope" (Romans 15:4).

No human word can match the power of the Word of God. As a young preacher, I was trained in all aspects of church work by Jim Bill McInteer. A part of this training involved shadowing McInteer as he did his work. This is how I learned the power of the Bible in the daily work of a church leader.

When he paid a visit to a member's home or to a hospital room, he normally did three things: He would pay attention to the person, close with a word of prayer, and have a time of Scripture reading. He knew the power of letting God speak to His people.

The Need for Equipment

The Bible is our primary resource for correcting and for encouraging God's people. It is also the primary resource to equip God's people in the Lord's service: "All Scripture is breathed out by God and profitable for teaching, for reproof, for correction, and for training in righteousness, that the man of God may be complete, equipped for every good work" (2 Timothy 3:16-17).

In assessing and addressing the needs of the church, too often congregations bow their knees to the Baals of psychology, marketing or entertainment. Instead of listening to the fickle gods of this age, the church needs to listen to unchanging God who speaks in Scripture.

The work of church leaders was described by Paul in Ephesians 4:12-14:

> Equip the saints for the work of ministry, for building up the body of Christ, until we all attain to the unity of the faith and of the knowledge of the Son of God, to mature manhood, to the measure of the stature of the fullness of Christ, so that we may no longer be children, tossed to and fro by the waves and carried about by every wind of doctrine, by human cunning, by craftiness in deceitful schemes.

Effectiveness in the Lord's church is primarily submission to the Lord's truth. Listening to God as He speaks to us through Scripture, we can be prepared to identify the spiritual needs of God's people and to address these needs as God directs.

Our fellowship grows from a shared commitment to God's truth and a shared experience of God's grace: "So we, though many, are one body in Christ, and individually members of one another" (Romans 12:5). We must not let our business in church work overshadow our work of exalting the Lord through His church – "Him we proclaim, warning everyone and teaching everyone with all wisdom, that we may present everyone mature in Christ" (Colossians 1:28). The truths of Scripture, instilled into the hearts of Christians, bind us together in a common cause and empower us for every good work.

For
REFLECTION

1. *How do we get into trouble focusing on wants instead of needs?*

2. *Why does human opinion often identify as needs things that are not addressed in Scripture?*

3. *How does "oiling squeaky wheels" reward people for being complainers?*

4. *How does a person balance the needs of an individual with the needs of a group?*

NOTES: _____

_____

_____

_____

_____

_____

_____

_____

_____

_____

_____

_____

_____

_____

_____

_____

_____

_____

_____

_____

_____

9

Effective
COMMUNICATION

Jesus Christ provided a flawless pattern of effectiveness. Although we will never come close to reaching His perfect standard, Christ is the example that guides our way. Humbly recognizing our limitations, we should want to be like Jesus.

We look to the pattern of godly effectiveness preeminently displayed in the story of Jesus recounted by the four gospels. We also learn about our Lord in His continued work through the church, described in the book of Acts and in the epistles. In anticipation, the story of the Savior is also revealed in great detail through the Hebrew scriptures, and many lessons come from the messianic prophecies as well.

Christ is the One speaking in Isaiah 50:4, describing His excellence in communication, a standard to which we should all aspire: "The Lord GOD has given me the tongue of those who are taught, that I may know how to sustain with a word him who is weary. Morning by morning he awakens; he awakens my ear to hear as those who are taught."

What a blessing to have the gift of powerful speaking and of insightful listening. The ability to appropriately convey ideas and, more important, to accurately understand the ideas of others are keys to achievement in every area of life.

Communication as Fellowship

The work and worship of the church, companionship among friends, and love in a family all exist within the context of communication. Fellowship requires a shared understanding, and fellowship cannot exist without communication.

Our relationship with God is based on the Lord's gracious communication with us: "Long ago, at many times and in many ways, God spoke to our fathers by the prophets, but in these last days he has spoken to us by his Son, whom he appointed the heir of all things, through whom also he created the world" (Hebrews 1:1-2).

Without this shared understanding of truth, there could be no way of salvation. Our fellowship with God is grounded in a process of communication, which the Lord provided in love.

A failure in communication causes problems in every area of life. In the church, the shift away from doctrinal content to mere entertainment diminishes communication. Consider music in the church for example. In Colossians 3:16, Paul described the importance of doctrinal content in church music: "Let the word of Christ dwell in you richly, teaching and admonishing one another in all wisdom, singing psalms and hymns and spiritual songs, with thankfulness in your hearts to God."

As the focus of music becomes entertainment rather than instruction, communication diminishes and relationships suffer. One of the flaws of instrumental music is its replacing content with entertainment and substituting aesthetics for communication.

Likewise, when the focus of a congregation becomes institutional rather than relational, there is a simultaneous shift away from meaningful communication. Too often elders become distant boards of directors rather than leaders of a church family. Deacons fall into serving programs rather than serving people. Likewise, preachers become company spokesmen rather than evangelists.

Often, with an institutional focus the church will be drowning in slogans, clichés, mission statements and other verbiage. There is, however, a marked difference between pouring out words and effective communication.

We should remember Jesus' warning: "I tell you, on the day of judgment people will give account for every careless word they speak, for by your words you will be justified, and by your words you will be condemned" (Matthew 12:36-37).

Christians must recognize the importance of sound communication.

The shared understanding it brings knits lives together to the glory of God. Good communication promotes healthy fellowship, and poor communication warns of a dysfunctional fellowship.

Effective Communication for Christians

Effective communication is a process not an event. Excellence in communication develops over time. Three considerations guide Christians in developing the ability to communicate effectively.

First, we must be mindful of the importance of communication and deliberate in how we communicate. Second, we need to recognize the dynamics at work in each situation and adapt our communication appropriately. Finally, we must find the balance between an effective economy of words and the need for effective reinforcement.

These three central considerations move us forward, following the example of Jesus Christ. Let's review each in turn.

Be Thoughtful

Have we set a priority on effective communication? Excellence in any area of life is usually a conscious choice. Agreeing with Solomon that "a word fitly spoken is like apples of gold in a setting of silver" (Proverbs 25:11), we must take thought in how to aptly communicate.

Beginning the process of communication, we must be thoughtful about the purpose of our communication. Unless we have a goal in mind, we court disaster. As Solomon warned:

Effective communication is a process not an event.

> The words of a wise man's mouth win him favor, but the lips of a fool consume him. The beginning of the words of his mouth is foolishness, and the end of his talk is evil madness. A fool multiplies words, though no man knows what is to be, and who can tell him what will be after him? (Ecclesiastes 10:12-14)

The best way to avoid multiplying useless words is to have a clear purpose in your communication. Thoughtful purpose also extends to our plan of how to proceed in communicating once we have set our purpose.

When I was being certified in first aid by the Red Cross, my instructor stressed the need for thoughtful consideration in any emergency situation. Too often when faced with a health emergency, people embrace a "don't just stand there, do something" line of attack. Rather, the Red Cross trains responders to use the opposite approach. "Sometimes it's more appropriate to not do anything, but just stand there" is their touchstone.

We can no more unsay a word than we can uncut a board.

A sober second thought can make all the difference in communication as well. Following the process described in Judges 19:30, one should "consider it, take counsel, and speak" in establishing a communications goal.

The carpenter's motto – "measure twice, cut once" – applies in working with words as much as it applies in working with wood. We can no more unsay a word than we can uncut a board. Be thoughtful in deciding what to say and in deciding how to say it.

Be Situational

Management theory in the past few decades has come to recognize the unique worth and personal dignity of individual men and women. Perhaps no one has brought the human element more clearly into focus than Kenneth Blanchard in his many popular books promoting "situational leadership."

In the church we must be more concerned with people than with processes, for servant leadership is relational rather than mechanical. By definition, concern for people is "situational." The Bible tells us "in humility [to] count others more significant than yourselves" (Philippians 2:3).

As servant leaders, we must frame our message in a way that honors the life situation of those who will receive the message. Colossians 4:6 makes this same point: "Let your speech always be gracious, seasoned with salt, so that you may know how you ought to answer each person."

People differ in many ways, and effective communication takes into account the life situations of individuals. Speech that is "seasoned with salt" takes into account differences in preferred learning styles, experience and expertise, perceived needs and countless other differences that may help sharpen the message. Be situational in crafting the message, and it will stand a much better chance of it being received.

Be Measured

In fourth grade I received an assignment to memorize a poem. My mother introduced me to "The Fool's Prayer" by Edward Rowland Sill. It is a story of a court jester – a "fool" – who offers a prayer of majestic wisdom. One stanza of this 19th-century poem asks: "The ill-timed truth we might have kept – / Who knows how sharp it pierced and stung? / The word we had not sense to say – / Who knows how grandly it had rung?"

Solomon reminds us there is "a time to keep silence, and a time to speak" (Ecclesiastes 3:7). Knowing how to measure our words is a foundational skill of spiritual effectiveness.

"When words are many, transgression is not lacking," Proverbs 10:19 warns, "but whoever restrains his lips is prudent." When a government prints more and more currency, its value drops proportionally. Likewise, the value of words declines with excessive verbosity.

Jesus taught the value of an economy of words in keeping our relationship with God authentic: "And when you pray, do not heap up empty phrases as the Gentiles do, for they think that they will be heard for their many words" (Matthew 6:7).

"Whoever restrains his words has knowledge, and he who has a cool spirit is a man of understanding. Even a fool who keeps silent is considered wise; when he closes his lips, he is deemed intelligent" (Proverbs 17:27-28). A measured approach, exercising a judicious stewardship of communication, gives your message added weight and value.

A measured approach gives your message added weight and value.

Effective communication requires insight to frame a message and skill to deliver it. However, delivering a message is only half of the work of communication. An adept communicator must also be an astute listener. Listening shows the value we place on another person, and through listening, we can become more productive in all areas of our lives.

Listening as an Act of Love

God's love for us is inseparably linked to His listening to us. As Psalm 119:149 implores, "Hear my voice according to your steadfast love; O LORD, according to your justice give me life." In the same way, our listening to the Lord reflects our love for God.

A reciprocal listening is fundamental to the covenant of grace. We listen to God, and God listens to us. If however, we stop listening to God, then God will no longer listen to us:

> And the word of the LORD came to Zechariah, saying, "Thus says the LORD of hosts, Render true judgments, show kindness and mercy to one another, do not oppress the widow, the fatherless, the sojourner, or the poor, and let none of you devise evil against another in your heart." But they refused to pay attention and turned a stubborn shoulder and stopped their ears that they might not hear. They made their hearts diamond-hard lest they should hear the law and the words that the LORD of hosts had sent by his Spirit through the former prophets. Therefore great anger came from the LORD of hosts. "As I called, and they would not hear, so they called, and I would not hear," says the LORD of hosts. (Zechariah 7:8-13)

Our love for God causes us to listen to God. This communication is essential to our salvation. "Therefore we must pay much closer attention to what we have heard, lest we drift away from it" (Hebrews 2:1).

Just as we listen to God because we love Him, the value we place on other people shows in the way we listen to them. President Theodore Roosevelt said, "Nobody cares how much you know, until they know how much you care." Effectiveness depends on seeing the value of each person and permitting each to participate in building a shared understanding.

Years ago, Ira North built a successful work with the Madison congregation with an approach that valued each person by listening to them. One of his famous catchphrases was "At the Madison Church of Christ, everybody has his say, but nobody gets his way – all the time." Listening is an act of love we learn from God and an essential tool for effective Christians.

Listening as Christian Service

Social psychologists often observe there is not as strong a correlation between measured intelligence and success as one would think. The CEOs of major corporations, for example, average only slightly higher scores on standardized tests than the general population.

Why do geniuses often fail to reach the top? Because, typically, very bright individuals are accustomed to being right, so they fail to ask other people for their opinions. No matter how bright a person may be, he or she is never right all the time.

"Without counsel plans fail," Proverbs 15:22 warns, "but with many advisers they succeed." It is arrogant for any of us to imagine we have all the insight needed in every possible situation. Effective leaders must cultivate the humility of listening and recognizing that we all can benefit from a broader perspective.

God has entrusted each Christian with a wide range of gifts and opportunities for which we are held accountable. Leaders in the church are called to be productive stewards of God's grace. Adept

Adept listening enhances our skills in God's service.

listening enhances our skills and improves our productivity in God's service. "Listen to advice and accept instruction, that you may gain wisdom in the future" (Proverbs 19:20).

By listening, Christian leaders can improve every aspect of their work in servant leadership. Attentiveness is, in itself, a task of servant leadership. Notice how prominently attentiveness factors into the admonition given in Acts 20:28-31 by Paul to the Ephesian elders:

> Pay careful attention to yourselves and to all the flock, in which the Holy Spirit has made you overseers, to care for the church of God, which he obtained with his own blood. I know that after my departure fierce wolves will come in among you, not sparing the flock; and from among your own selves will arise men speaking twisted things, to draw away the disciples after them. Therefore be alert, remembering that for three years I did not cease night or day to admonish everyone with tears.

A Christian cannot effectively serve God's people unless he knows God's people. All Christians are to "rejoice with those who rejoice, weep with those who weep" (Romans 12:15), and we are to "bear one another's burdens, and so fulfill the law of Christ" (Galatians 6:2). The attentiveness of an effective Christian, however, must go beyond emotional support. Servant leadership carries with it the spiritual responsibility of doctrinal awareness.

Christians must appreciate the importance of both powerful speaking and insightful listening. Developing the ability to appropriately convey ideas and accurately understand the ideas of others enhances every aspect of service to God.

For
REFLECTION

1. *How has the electronic media affected communication for better or worse?*

2. *Can you think of an example of a time when you thought you were clear in your communication but were still misunderstood?*

3. *How can we improve communication in our congregations?*

4. *How do our communication priorities reflect our spiritual commitments?*

NOTES: _____

_____

_____

_____

_____

_____

_____

_____

_____

_____

_____

_____

_____

_____

_____

_____

_____

10

Effective
DISCIPLESHIP

Members of the church are called to apply themselves in many areas of work, and a common thread running through the whole pattern of this work is discipleship. In Matthew 28:18-20, Jesus Christ commissioned His church to develop disciples as its central mission:

> And Jesus came and said to them, "All authority in heaven and on earth has been given to me. Go therefore and make disciples of all nations, baptizing them in the name of the Father and of the Son and of the Holy Spirit, teaching them to observe all that I have commanded you. And behold, I am with you always, to the end of the age."

The church is constituted, at its very core, to be a learning organization. The church is in the business of making disciples. By definition, a disciple is one who develops competency under the guidance of a master. In the church, our Master is Jesus Christ. Following the Lord is a developmental process that brings His disciples into a greater conformity to His example.

An Invitation to Learn

The Lord's invitation has always been an invitation to learn: "Come to me, all who labor and are heavy laden, and I will give you rest. Take my yoke upon you, and learn from me, for I am gentle and lowly in heart, and you will find rest for your souls. For my yoke is easy, and my burden is light" (Matthew 11:28-30). To be a disciple is to be one who learns from Jesus Christ.

This emphasis on learning extends through the entire pattern for the church laid out in the New Testament. The Bible describes effectiveness in the church primarily as managing the learning process, embracing the truth of God, and bringing this truth into the lives of faithful men and women. In Ephesians 4:11-14, Paul highlighted the importance of this developmental process in the church:

> And he gave the apostles, the prophets, the evangelists, the shepherds and teachers, to equip the saints for the work of ministry, for building up the body of Christ, until we all attain to the unity of the faith and of the knowledge of the Son of God, to mature manhood, to the measure of the stature of the fullness of Christ, so that we may no longer be children, tossed to and fro by the waves and carried about by every wind of doctrine, by human cunning, by craftiness in deceitful schemes.

Notice that "building up the body of Christ" is not something done by marketing the church to the world. The developmental work of the church is internal. The goal of the church is to equip the saints with spiritual competency. Through this developmental process, the work of ministry is accomplished.

The goal of the church is to equip the saints with spiritual competency.

Also notice the implicit order of priorities in the discipleship-development process. The faithful Christian places God first, others second and himself last.

Placing God first in the process keeps the church faithful to God's Word. This priority provides a zeal for doctrinal integrity. To be a disciple requires authentically following the Master, seeking in every way to follow His direction.

The example and teachings of Jesus lead us to make other people a priority. Our Lord commissioned the church to make disciples, setting the priority on the development of individual

Christians under the authority of Jesus Christ. Placing others before yourself recognizes the critical need for humble service in the church. Sadly, however, this biblical emphasis is abandoned when Christians follow differing agendas.

Focus on Discipleship

Congregations devote much time to providing excellent programs for religious instruction and edification. At best, our efforts produce mixed results for the effort expended. Too often we fail to remember that people learn as individuals and not as a class or as a group.

The increased staffing of congregations with paid professionals has often pulled the church away from the New Testament pattern of discipleship development. Paid professionals are normally assessed on short-term and superficial results, through which they justify larger salaries and expanded budgets.

The result of this approach is often an organizational superstructure that takes on a life of its own, apart from the members of the church. The individual members become a means toward the end of building the program.

In contrast, the New Testament pattern of discipleship development does not proceed in the refinement of elaborate programs but in lives that are equipped to follow the Master. The biblical approach builds a relational infrastructure that develops the competencies of each member. The biblical approach is low-budget and long-term.

Discipleship, the development of Christian competency, is a learning process. It is a journey rather than a destination. However adept we may become in our service to the Lord, we can always improve. The example of Jesus Christ is a beacon, guiding us ever onward.

Competency in Christian service requires developing a combination of attitudes, knowledge and skills. Attitudes are most important and are most difficult to acquire. Often a new attitude must replace an old attitude before skills or knowledge can be used.

It is only within the context of relationship that we are able to detect the attitudinal needs of church members and know how to effect needed change. This emphasis on collaborative development is central to the New Testament pattern for the church. None of us has attained perfection, but together we are moving forward.

In Philippians 3:12-17, Paul described this journey and the fellowship we share in moving one another along:

Not that I have already obtained this or am already perfect, but I press on to make it my own, because Christ Jesus has made me his own. Brothers, I do not consider that I have made it my own. But one thing I do: forgetting what lies behind and straining forward to what lies ahead, I press on toward the goal for the prize of the upward call of God in Christ Jesus. Let those of us who are mature think this way, and if in anything you think otherwise, God will reveal that also to you. Only let us hold true to what we have attained. Brothers, join in imitating me, and keep your eyes on those who walk according to the example you have in us.

An understanding of Christian growth as a continual process rather than a finite event, keeps our focus on the development of people rather than on the building of programs. This discipleship model guides the learning process in a wide range of development opportunities in the church.

Recognizing discipleship as a journey rather than an event, we can readily identify ways in which every aspect of church life has a developmental component. Not only in worship services and in Bible classes but also through informal discussions and godly example, the church makes disciples as it instills and develops spiritual competency among Christians.

Four Facets
of Discipleship Development

Every opportunity for spiritual development contributes to the learning process in at least one of four ways. First, and most basic, discipleship occurs as the need for greater competency is established. Often we need to be stirred out of smugness. The primary message of Jesus was "Repent!" Unless we see the need for spiritual development, we will not embrace the path of discipleship.

Second, discipleship occurs as Christian doctrine is confirmed and is reaffirmed. Second Timothy 3:16-17 reminds us of the need for biblical content to properly develop disciples: "All Scripture is breathed out by God and profitable for teaching, for reproof, for correction, and for training in righteousness, that the man of God may be competent, equipped for every good work." Christian competency rests on understanding and applying the Word of God. Without an understanding of Scripture, there can be no discipleship.

Third, discipleship occurs as the drive for progress is fueled by motivation. There is an emotive spark required both to bring a person to faith in Christ and to encourage God's people to keep on keeping on. While Christian motivation must always embody the truth of Scripture, it is more than a mere repetition of facts.

Fourth, discipleship occurs as the discipline of continual practice shapes a Christian's attitudes, skills and knowledge over time.

Opportunities for Discipleship

We need to consider various opportunities for discipleship. Sadly, many commonplace opportunities are overlooked, while many obscure practices gain favor among us. Discipleship has been the focus of many aberrant teachings among professing Christians. We need to learn to be more discerning.

Simply asking why can save us from much error.

In a class at Emory University, I learned about a "Plan Meets Need" analysis in public policy debate. This asks the fundamental question: Why are you proposing this approach, and does your plan meet our needs? Simply asking why can save us from much error.

Some in the church tout the practice of "prayer vigils" as a source of spiritual strength. This idea – borrowed from Catholic mysticism – puts forward that prayer is more potent if conducted round-the-clock. Others, in a similar quest for radical discipleship, advocate skipping a meal and donating a commensurate amount to some worthy cause.

A moment's reflection shows no correlation between the prescribed activity and any proposed benefit. Such super-spiritual theatrics are all sizzle and no steak. I can pray just as effectively during normal waking hours as I can in the dead of night, and the small sum I may donate to a proposed charity has no connection to whether I skip a meal.

We should be asking, why will the proposed activity develop the needed attitudes, knowledge or skills to enhance discipleship? In contrast to odd and extreme approaches to discipleship, the

Lord's church has been blessed with many ordinary yet neglected opportunities to make individuals effective disciples of Jesus Christ.

In Worship

The most profound and overlooked opportunity for discipleship is the weekly worship service. Much currently done in the religious world during the worship service is experience-based rather than content-based. The driving force is the experience the individual feels rather than the validity of that experience. In contrast, Jesus called us to worship "in spirit and truth" (John 4:24, cf. Matthew 15:8-9). When worship is conducted according to the pattern laid out in Scripture, the effect upon the worshipers is profound.

> *When worship is conducted according to the pattern laid out in Scripture, the effect upon the worshipers is profound.*

Following the pattern of Scripture, preaching will have as its main point the salvation provided in Jesus Christ. Paul described his preaching in 1 Corinthians 1:18-24:

> For the word of the cross is folly to those who are perishing, but to us who are being saved it is the power of God. For it is written, "I will destroy the wisdom of the wise, and the discernment of the discerning I will thwart." Where is the one who is wise? Where is the scribe? Where is the debater of this age? Has not God made foolish the wisdom of the world? For since, in the wisdom of God, the world did not know God through wisdom, it pleased God through the folly of what we preach to save those who believe. For Jews demand signs and Greeks seek wisdom, but we preach Christ crucified, a stumbling block to Jews and folly to Gentiles, but to those who are called, both Jews and Greeks, Christ the power of God and the wisdom of God.

Far too many sermons are filled with empty psycho-babble and unscriptural platitudes. Such preaching (when done well) can entertain, but only biblical preaching will make disciples. This point was driven home by Christ in the Great Commission. Following His guidance and the example of His apostles, we should preach "Christ the power of God and the wisdom of God" (1 Corinthians 18:24).

Beyond preaching, the Word of God should inform and direct every facet of worship. Rather than obsessing over the aesthetics of our singing, we should make sure its content is empowered by Scripture.

"Let the word of Christ dwell in you richly," Paul wrote in Colossians 3:16, "teaching and admonishing one another in all wisdom, singing psalms and hymns and spiritual songs, with thankfulness in your hearts to God." Singing should provide mutual edification, as we all are brought into harmony with the lordship of Christ when His Word dwells in us richly.

Each first day of the week, the Lord's church is privileged to observe the Lord's Supper. The pattern of Scripture is clear. This observance is to be done in the setting of the gathered church as a proclamation of the gospel: "For as often as you eat this bread and drink the cup, you proclaim the Lord's death until he comes" (1 Corinthians 11:26).

This time of shared reflection keeps all faithful Christians in alignment with the way of Christ. "Let a person examine himself, then," Paul continued, "and so eat of the bread and drink of the cup" (1 Corinthians 11:28). The intersection of God's truth with an examination of our lives is the essence of discipleship.

In Christian Service

Just as God has given a pattern for the worship of the church, He has also given a pattern for the work of the church. We are edified when we follow God's pattern in worship. We will also be blessed when we follow His pattern in doing His work.

The intersection of God's truth with an examination of our lives is the essence of discipleship.

God's work is to be done by God's people gathered into congregations and according to God's plan. One of many evils of unscriptural plans for church organization is they consistently move the focus of work away from the congregation into a distant bureaucracy. Losing the immediacy of involvement, members of the church lose a valuable opportunity for training in righteousness.

In sharp distinction, the biblical pattern given by God to do His work keeps the Lord's people in a discipleship mode. Christians are built up in their faith as they participate in the work of a congregation and see active faith displayed by others. Elders are called to be "examples to the flock," and evangelists are to be "a model of good works" (1 Peter 5:3; Titus 2:7).

Beyond what is said from the pulpit or in a classroom, discipleship occurs within the varied opportunities of service done by members of a congregation under the oversight of their leaders.

Discipleship is neither reserved for an elite few nor for new converts. Every Christian, from the newly baptized to the aged saint, needs a commitment to spiritual growth. We should have in our hearts the aspiration expressed by Paul: "I press on toward the goal for the prize of the upward call of God in Christ Jesus" (Philippians 3:14). The more we experience the truth of Christ in our lives, the more we will be made over into effective servants in His image.

For
REFLECTION

1. *How can training in Christian service, such as visitation, become part of the work of the church?*

2. *What happens to a congregation when discipleship is ignored?*

3. *Can someone be an effective elder or evangelist and not toil in the various works of the congregation?*

4. *How is following God's pattern in the work and worship of the church an essential aspect of discipleship?*

NOTES: _____

_____

_____

_____

_____

_____

_____

_____

_____

_____

_____

_____

_____

_____

_____

_____

_____

_____

_____

11

Effective
REPRESENTATION

Wearing the name "Christian" makes us accountable for the way in which we present ourselves before a watching world. This is true in secular organizations, and it is true in the Lord's church.

Going through training for new Boy Scout leaders, we were taught about honoring the scout uniform – when it could be worn and, more important, when it could not.

Scout leaders are supposed to wear their uniforms when transporting youth to and from scouting events. However, wearing the uniform while traveling brought some restrictions. We were told, for example, never to accept seating in the bar area of a restaurant while wearing a Scout uniform, for the Boy Scouts of America does not promote drinking alcohol.

As a Christian, especially one who embraces a position of leadership, a uniform must be worn that cannot be removed and must never be dishonored: "For as many of you as were baptized into Christ have put on Christ" (Galatians 3:27).

Discipleship Is in the Details

"You were bought with a price," 1 Corinthians 6:20 reminds us. We do not want to dishonor the Lord who saved us. Remembering to whom we belong will make major changes in the way we present ourselves, both to the outside world and to those within the church.

Our lives, however, are not mainly made up of big things but of countless small things. This moment-by-moment reality means letting the love of Christ guide us, even in the smallest matter: "One who is faithful in a very little

Remembering to whom we belong will make major changes in the way we present ourselves.

is also faithful in much, and one who is dishonest in a very little is also dishonest in much" (Luke 16:10). One small thing that speaks volumes about us is the way we attend to dress and grooming.

Beginning in the 1960s, there arose among the youth of Western nations a counterculture, the badge of which is carelessness about personal appearance. Ironically, many spend much time, effort and money in their quest to look cheap, casual and grimy.

But we should not be concerned with outward appearance, should we? You cannot judge a book by its cover. Well, many do select books because of their covers.

My friends at the Gospel Advocate Co. put much effort into regularly producing a catalog of the materials they offer for sale. This catalog could just be an inventory list with the name, author and price displayed in uninterrupted columns lining page after page. But when you open the Gospel Advocate catalog, many of the products are pictured. A picture, so they say, is worth a thousand words.

The power of nonverbal communication should not surprise us. Educators have long known that students learn far more from seeing and joining in than by reading and listening alone. So it should not surprise us that how a Christian presents himself is a large part of his effectiveness.

A runaway bestseller in the 1970s was John T. Molloy's *Dress for Success*. Molloy, a social scientist, used controlled research to prove that what you wear influences how you are perceived and the results you produce.

Two men stand before a congregation. Each delivers a message taken from the Word of God. One man wears blue jeans and a T-shirt. He has dressed to suit himself. The second man wears a coat and tie. His careful selection of clothing bespeaks a respect for the importance of his message, an appreciation for those listening to him, and a humility in fulfilling the office to which he has been called.

Bob Gibbs, who served for many years as an elder in Ohio, was, in his professional life, a successful executive for Ashland Oil Co.'s chemical division. As Bob traveled to meet with the employees reporting to him across a multistate region, he insisted that "when they came to work, they dressed for work."

When John G. Roberts became Chief Justice of the Supreme Court, nothing in the Constitution required him to don a black robe. He could have appeared in jeans and a sweatshirt. But he would not have been taken seriously. He would have disgraced his office. He would have disgraced himself. He would have been ineffectual. Roberts' intellectual brilliance would have been beside the point. As the title of Roger Ailes' 1988 book famously noted, *You Are the Message.*

When schools want to raise standards of academics and behavior, a universally productive tool is adopting a school uniform. A uniform places an emphasis on the importance of the work being done, rather than on the particular person doing the work.

Of course, we know formality and informality of dress are cultural trends. But being a trend does not make something right, expedient or effective. The need for effective service calls us to look beyond arrogant self-expression. Christians must stay focused on their task of service and on those God has called them to serve.

The Hallmark of Christian Effectiveness

Suitable dress and appearance for leaders in the Lord's church is only an outward sign of an inward grace. The message we communicate – the words we choose, the clothes we wear, the actions we take – must be consistently brought together by the gospel of Jesus Christ.

Jim Bill McInteer served as the preacher for the West End congregation in Nashville, Tenn., for more than three decades. He will always be my benchmark for effective preaching. McInteer's success as a preacher flowed from the way he kept a servant's perspective from the pulpit.

Each Sunday, before McInteer greeted the congregation he read a short message to himself, which he had affixed to the pulpit: "Before you are the people of God, treat them accordingly." This placing of God and others ahead of one's self is the hallmark of Christian servant leadership.

Our reliance on God maximizes our influence with other people to His glory and for their betterment. As in Colossians 1:28, Paul wrote: "Him we proclaim, warning everyone and teaching everyone with all wisdom, that we may present everyone mature in Christ." Our obedience to God in Jesus Christ is the context in which the church "builds itself up in love" (Ephesians 4:16).

Christian leaders are doing God's work as they serve the church. Ultimately, through our efforts, it is God at work in the church (Philippians 2:13). In the same way, we are God's representatives to the world.

The Responsibility of All Christians

Jesus Christ is the true light that has entered the world (John 1:9). While Jesus told us "I am the light of the world" (John 8:12), He told His disciples: "You are the light of the world. A city set on a hill cannot be hidden. ... Let your light shine before others, so that they may see your good works and give glory to your Father who is in heaven" (Matthew 5:14-16). It is "through the church the manifold wisdom of God" is displayed in the present age (Ephesians 3:10).

As Teresa of Avila wrote in the 16th century:

> Christ has no body now on earth but yours; no hands but yours; no feet but yours. Yours are the eyes through which the compassion of Christ must look out on the world. Yours are the feet with which He is to go about doing good. Yours are the hands with which He is to bless His people.

Our work in the world is in the name of Jesus and for His sake. As the body of Christ, we are His agency in this world. On this basis, we are to conduct ourselves toward outsiders in wisdom.

The responsibility to represent Christ to the world belongs to all Christians, especially to those who are in positions of leadership. Elders, for example, "must be well thought of by outsiders" (1 Timothy 3:7). Christians must continually consider the way their reputations reflect on the church and on our Lord.

Remember Who Is in Charge

Jesus Christ, our example, shows what it means to serve under orders of delegated authority. "So Jesus said to them ... 'I do nothing on my own authority, but speak just as the Father taught me' " (John 8:28).

Our position as representatives is simultaneously restrictive and empowering. "For the love of Christ controls us," Paul noted in 2 Corinthians 5:14. We are not free to launch out on our own, but in obedient faith we are "not to go beyond what is written" (1 Corinthians 4:6). However, within the bounds of the revealed truth that constrains us, God has granted us great authority. "Whoever speaks," 1 Peter 4:11 instructs, should do so "as one who speaks oracles of God."

> *All Christians are acting under God's authority and are empowered by that authority.*

Of course, divine empowerment is most fully seen in Jesus Christ and His authoritative representatives: the apostles. Delegated authority, however, is not limited to the Lord and the apostles. Everyone who is entrusted with the message from God goes with the authority inherent in that message.

For example, consider our Lord's description of the authority enjoyed by the 72 disciples He sent out to preach: "The one who hears you hears me, and the one who rejects you rejects me, and the one who rejects me rejects him who sent me" (Luke 10:16). Jesus was not describing the authority of the apostles. He showed that all Christians are acting under God's authority and are empowered by that authority.

If Christians accurately teach the message of God's Word, they are empowered by God's authority. This authority is seen in elders who rule in God's church (1 Timothy 5:17) and in evangelists, like Titus, whom Paul commanded to "exhort and rebuke with all authority" (Titus 2:15). Our authority as Christians is empowered by our relationship with Jesus Christ: "I am the vine; you are the branches. Whoever abides in me and I in him, he it is that bears much fruit, for apart from me you can do nothing" (John 15:5).

Faithfully representing Jesus Christ in the church and in the world, we continue with the full authority of Jesus Christ. Apart from this authority revealed to us in Scripture, there is no power in the church. Apart from Jesus, we can do nothing.

As representatives of Jesus, we see that all of life – every moment – may be Christ-affirming or Christ-denying. "And whatever you do, in word or deed, do everything in the name of the Lord Jesus, giving thanks to God the Father through him" (Colossians 3:17). The warp and the woof of Christian effectiveness is remembering who is in charge.

For
REFLECTION

1. *Is there a danger of hypocrisy if we are concerned with how people view us?*

2. *How do you think men who lead in worship should dress?*

3. *What image do non-Christians in your community have of your congregation?*

4. *Is paying attention to outward appearance superficial?*

NOTES: _____

_____

_____

_____

_____

_____

_____

_____

_____

_____

_____

_____

_____

_____

_____

_____

_____

12

Effective
GUIDANCE

While a concern for effectiveness is often preoccupied with a person's role in an organization, the Bible presents effectiveness in terms of the effect we have in the lives of others. We see this approach in Jesus investing Himself in the lives of the chosen disciples, through whom He expanded His influence in the building of His church.

Tolbert Fanning was a towering influence building the church in the South. While well-known as a preacher and a writer, Fanning's greatest legacy was the investment he made of himself in the lives of the young men under his influence. Fanning's work blessed generations of Christians through the ministry of the young men he equipped for service at Franklin College.

Fanning's protégé, David Lipscomb, studied at Franklin College and served with Fanning as co-editor of the *Gospel Advocate*. When Lipscomb became sole editor, he used his role as editor to develop a circle of younger men who would serve the church far beyond his own life and work.

Biblical Guidance From Godly Leaders

An essential element of relational leadership is providing appropriate guidance. God's leadership in our lives is often described by Scripture in terms of guidance. As Isaiah 42:16 tells us:

> And I will lead the blind in a way that they do not know, in paths that they have not known I will guide them. I will turn the darkness before them into light, the rough places into level ground. These are the things I do, and I do not forsake them.

When in worship we sing the hymn "Savior, Like a Shepherd Lead Us," we recognize God's saving work engages our lives through His directive Word. Biblical leadership always takes its cue from this truth and seeks to apply God's Word in the lives of God's people.

Scripture uses the words "guidance" and "counsel" interchangeably. In Proverbs 11:14, for example, we read: "Where there is no guidance, a people falls, but in an abundance of counselors there is safety." A counselor is one who provides guidance. Unfortunately, the current practice of psychological counseling has obscured the importance of spiritual counseling.

Christian counseling guides an individual into successfully following the will of God.

While clinical psychology may be appropriate to help people with a wide range of mental health issues, it is a mistake to read into the Bible secular theories created almost 2,000 years after the time of Christ and His apostles. Psychoanalysis, as a way of treating neuroses, was shaped by a man named Sigmund Freud at the turn of the last century and has nothing to do with the application of Scripture in the lives of God's people.

Counseling, as described in Scripture, guides individuals to apply the will of God in their lives and in every aspect of their service to God. Effectively encouraging human potential in achievement of the Lord's work is a worthy goal. No resource exists to guide humans in making their potential greater than the revealed will of God. Our relationship with God unlocks our greatest potential and identifies the highest goals we should aspire to achieve. In short, the Bible tells us what we ought to do and how we ought to do it.

Christian counseling, properly understood, guides an individual into successfully following the will of God. From this standpoint, the Bible tells us a great deal about the sort of counseling needed to guide individuals in their walk with God.

God's counsel is part of His providential care. "I will instruct you and teach you in the way you should go," God promised in Psalm 32:8, "I will counsel you with my eye upon you." When people seek a relationship with God apart from God's self-revelation in Scripture, they end up replacing the God of Scripture with a god of their own imagination.

God's active involvement in leading His people cannot be severed from His guidance given in Scripture. As the hymn goes, "When we walk with the Lord / In the light of His Word, / What a glory He sheds on our way!"

Counsel severed from God's revealed will leads to darkness rather than to light. As Job lamented, " 'Who is this that hides counsel with knowledge?' Therefore I have uttered what I did not understand, things too wonderful for me, which I did not know" (Job 42:3).

We need to learn the lesson Job learned – but hopefully without going through what he went through to learn it. We need to rely on what God has said and not on human speculation. "With God are wisdom and might; he has counsel and understanding" (Job 12:13).

The Bible Is Sufficient

Harvey Floyd, a former Bible professor at Lipscomb University, told a story of a hostess who prepared a lavish meal at great expense. She provided her guests course after course of the finest foods. Multiple appetizers, soups and salads, fresh baked breads, and numerous side dishes accompanied the delicious main dish.

Finally, the guests were treated to dessert with a choice of freshly prepared cakes and pies. Floyd then asked what we would think of a guest who, finishing this meal, would look to his hostess and say, "I'd like something else."

In exactly this way, we have received the fullness of God's revelation through the inspired writers and, most important, in the example and teachings of our Savior (Hebrews 1:1-3). Yet we say to God, "I'd like something else."

A lack of faith is the root cause for rejecting the inerrancy of Scripture. A lack of faith is also the root cause for rejecting the sufficiency of Scripture. It boils down to a simple question: Do you believe God knows what He is talking about?

Paul's answer to this question resonates in the words of 2 Timothy 3:16-17: "All Scripture is breathed out by God and profitable for teaching, for reproof, for correction, and for training in righteousness, that the man of God may be complete, equipped for every good work."

The inspiration of Scripture, meaning that every word of Scripture is a direct word from God, is the source not only of its authority but also of its ability. Notice the way Scripture may be used to counsel Christians in a wide range of life situations through teaching, reproof, correction and training in righteousness. The Word of God is sufficient to equip Christians in every good work.

Through Teaching

Christianity is a revealed religion. Unlike piecemeal human attempts to construct truth, the Christian faith is delivered in its entirety from God. In His Word, God provides all the guidance we need.

Philosophies such as Buddhism or Taoism are monumental works of human effort. Christianity is, from beginning to end, a work of God's grace. We do not manufacture truth; we receive it from God.

A thorough knowledge of Scripture is essential for every aspect of Christian leadership but especially as we venture to give guidance to others. When we guide people with our opinions rather than with the truths of Scripture, we stand in danger of usurping the place of God in directing His people.

> *We do not manufacture truth; we receive it from God.*

As with so many aspects of our lives, godly counsel is a matter of stewardship:

> As each has received a gift, use it to serve one another, as good stewards of God's varied grace: whoever speaks, as one who speaks oracles of God; whoever serves, as one who serves by the strength that God supplies – in order that in everything God may be glorified through Jesus Christ. To him belong glory and dominion forever and ever. Amen. (1 Peter 4:10-11)

Whenever possible, we should apply biblical truth when giving guidance. Better yet, we should teach others how to study and apply the truths of Scripture for themselves. We give glory to God when we point people to His truth rather than to our own cleverness.

When we are compelled to offer our own opinions, we must have humility in keeping our opinions separate from the Word of God. But before ever venturing into the realm of opinion, we should be diligent in looking to the Word of God. "A fool takes no pleasure in understanding," Proverbs 18:2 warns, "but only in expressing his opinion."

Through Reproof

"Reproof" is not a common English word. In 2 Timothy 3:16, the New International Version substitutes the word "rebuking." This substitution embraces ease of understanding at the expense

> *We give glory to God when we point people to His truth rather than to our own cleverness.*

of accuracy. Better is the longer paraphrase of the New Living Translation: "to make us realize what is wrong."

I am convinced a major reason for the lack of successful evangelism in the church today is our avoidance of reproof. We are not doing anyone a favor by pretending what is wrong is right.

In college, I studied piano under Francis Crutcher. Classically trained, she could play beautifully. I could not. Often, I could hear there was a problem with my music, but I needed her guidance to bring harmony to the discord of my playing. In much the same way, people feel the discord of their lives but cannot find harmony by themselves.

Serious thinkers have addressed this feeling of discord. Beginning with Søren Kierkegaard (1813–1855) in *The Concept of Anxiety*, a major theme of philosophy has been "angst," a vague yet intense and pervasive awareness of insecurity and fear. Philosophers have known something is wrong, but they have not provided resolution to the problem.

What philosophers discuss in their ivory towers, artists express in their varied craft. From *The Scream*, painted by Edvard Munch, to playwright Samuel Beckett's *Waiting for Godot* and even to the staccato lyrics of rap singers, a dark thread runs through the fabric of Western culture. Artists skillfully depict the abyss of despair but show no path of escape.

And what philosophers talk about and artists express, people are experiencing in lives of despair. This feeling of personal discord drives men and women to look for resolution. Unable to bear the gnawing feeling of brokenness, they numb themselves with drugs and alcohol. Unable to find meaning in life, they satiate themselves with materialism and permissiveness.

The tragedy of social and moral decay is a testimony of people trying to overcome the discord of their lives. But their brokenness prevents them finding resolution on their own.

It is human nature to want to go along and get along. The spirit of our age calls for tolerance and acceptance. In our hearts, however, we all know something is wrong. We need the honesty of God's reproof if we are ever to make things right.

Through Correction

Scripture does more than diagnose problems; it also prescribes remedies. Medical analogies are used throughout the Bible to describe the brokenness of our lives as something addressed by God's healing. It is often hard to hear the truth concerning the gravity of our condition, but hearing the truth and receiving God's correction is our only hope.

Attention to Scripture is the hope of dawn following a night of despair.

We must counsel people to look into the Word of God and then to make application to their lives. As James directs:

> Therefore put away all filthiness and rampant wickedness and receive with meekness the implanted word, which is able to save your souls. But be doers of the word, and not hearers only, deceiving yourselves. For if anyone is a hearer of the word and not a doer, he is like a man who looks intently at his natural face in a mirror. For he looks at himself and goes away and at once forgets what he was like. But the one who looks into the perfect law, the law of liberty, and perseveres, being no hearer who forgets but a doer who acts, he will be blessed in his doing. (James 1:21-25)

It is never an imposition to guide someone into greater conformity to the pattern of faith laid out in Scripture – "the implanted word, which is able to save your souls" (James 1:21). The Word of God, however, only has power as it is implanted. James used a term calling to mind Jesus' parable of the sower. The good seed of Scripture will only bear fruit in a properly prepared heart.

Christian leadership must guide individuals to correct their lives according to the Word of God. It is only through the Lord's revelation of grace that healing and wholeness will come to our lives. "He sent out his word and healed them," Psalm 107:20 reminds us, "and delivered them from their destruction."

Through Training in Righteousness

The correction provided through the application of Scripture in our lives is not just the laying aside of what is wrong but also the embracing of what is right. "So you also must consider yourselves dead to sin," Paul wrote in Romans 6:11, "and alive to God in Christ Jesus." Leaders in the church must guide people in the way of righteous living.

Walking in the light and being right with God in Jesus Christ can only come as we receive the guidance of God's Word directing our lives. This attention to Scripture is described as the hope of dawn following a night of despair. As Peter wrote:

> And we have the prophetic word more fully confirmed, to which you will do well to pay attention as to a lamp shining in a dark place, until the day dawns and the morning star rises in your hearts, knowing this first of all, that no prophecy of Scripture comes from someone's own interpretation. For no prophecy was ever produced by the will of man, but men spoke from God as they were carried along by the Holy Spirit. (2 Peter 1:19-21)

Follow the Pattern

When we lack faith in God, we doubt the sufficiency of His Word. We ask marketers and sociologists for counsel when we want the church to grow. We ask experts in entertainment for guidance when we want to enhance our worship.

We ask professionals trained in secular psychology for healing when we want to mend our broken lives. We ask management theorists for plans when we want to effectively do the Lord's work.

We consistently rely on the best and brightest ideas human wisdom can construct. Perhaps before taking counsel of all these experts, we should have taken counsel from God.

Lacking faith in God leads to doubts in the inspiration, authority and sufficiency of the Bible. This disregard for God's Word leads to a disregard for God's people. The same lack of faith that doubts God's competence to speak accurately in His Scripture also doubts God's competence to work effectively through His people.

Yet there is no pattern of righteousness apart from what we read in Scripture. Paying attention to the prophetic Word brings the hope of a new day. Applying the pattern of Scripture to our lives is essential if we want to follow the Savior. "Follow the pattern of the sound words that you have heard from me," Paul wrote in 2 Timothy 1:13, "in the faith and love that are in Christ Jesus."

Rejecting the Word of God leaves one in darkness. As God warned in Isaiah 8:20, "To the teaching and to the testimony! If they will not speak according to this word, it is because they have no dawn."

Christian effectiveness requires knowing the Word of God, applying it in our own lives, and guiding others to apply it in theirs. This approach is guaranteed to provide blessings in the Lord as He leads us in righteousness.

For
REFLECTION

1. *Is employing mental health professionals in the church any different from employing dental health professionals?*

2. *What is the primary difference between biblical counseling and secular psychology?*

3. *Is it presumptuous to offer advice to another Christian?*

4. *What is the role of evangelists and elders in counselling church members?*

NOTES: _____

_____

_____

_____

_____

_____

_____

_____

_____

_____

_____

_____

_____

_____

_____

_____

_____

_____

13

Effective
SERVICE

The Lord has encouraged and enabled each of us in God's service. Following the example of Christ, we should encourage and enable others in this same life of service. The Great Commission, recorded in Matthew 28:18-20, reads:

> And Jesus came and said to them, "All authority in heaven and on earth has been given to me. Go therefore and make disciples of all nations, baptizing them in the name of the Father and of the Son and of the Holy Spirit, teaching them to observe all that I have commanded you. And behold, I am with you always, to the end of the age."

Under the authority of Jesus Christ, we are called into service. This service consists of going and converting others into this same life of service. When one is baptized into Christ, he or she is consecrated in this great work. We are to make disciples who will do all the Lord has commanded.

Grace and Works

Sometime grace and works are discussed as if they were two points on the opposite end of a line. From this standpoint, any emphasis on grace diminishes an emphasis on works and any emphasis on works diminishes an emphasis on grace. The Bible, however, does not place grace and works in opposition to one another. Rather, in Scripture we find grace and works harmoniously interwoven, as in Ephesians 2:8-10:

> For by grace you have been saved through faith. And this is not your own doing; it is the gift of God, not a result of works, so that no one may boast. For we are his workmanship, created in Christ Jesus for good works, which God prepared beforehand, that we should walk in them.

When we are baptized into Christ, we are born into the family of God, and we are privileged to enter into His family business. Just as Jesus came into the world to do the Father's will, we should follow the example of our Savior in the obedience that comes from faith. This faithful service includes not only what we can do ourselves but also what we can encourage and enable others to do.

Our common salvation brings us together in a shared commitment of service, as Hebrews 10:19-25 says:

> Therefore, brothers, since we have confidence to enter the holy places by the blood of Jesus, by the new and living way that he opened for us through the curtain, that is, through his flesh, and since we have a great priest over the house of God, let us draw near with a true heart in full assurance of faith, with our hearts sprinkled clean from an evil conscience and our bodies washed with pure water. Let us hold fast the confession of our hope without wavering, for he who promised is faithful. And let us consider how to stir up one another to love and good works, not neglecting to meet together, as is the habit of some, but encouraging one another, and all the more as you see the Day drawing near.

Beginning with the truth of salvation, which was purchased by the blood of Christ and is received by baptism into Christ, the author of Hebrews called us to consecrate ourselves and to "consider how to stir up one another to love and good works."

Fellowship in Service

One of the great authors in the church is Jimmy Jividen. For decades, congregations have been blessed in the study of his book *Koinonia: A Contemporary Study of Church Fellowship.* In this study, Jividen unfolds many profound implications of one simple truth: As each of us is brought closer to God, we will also be brought closer to one another.

> *As each of us is brought closer to God, we will also be brought closer to one another.*

This truth changes the way we do the work of the church. As long as we view the good accomplished as God's work, we are able to share together in His service without concern over who will get the credit. Paul made this point to the church in Corinth:

> I planted, Apollos watered, but God gave the growth. So neither he who plants nor he who waters is anything, but only God who gives the growth. He who plants and he who waters are one, and each will receive his wages according to his labor. (1 Corinthians 3:6-8)

The good that any one of us does rests upon the enabling grace of God mediated through His church. Every Christian is trained and developed by other Christians, as we all are trained and developed by God through His Word and through the example of Jesus Christ. He encouraged His disciples to keep focused on the great work before them and to remember that any good we accomplish rests upon the work of others:

> Jesus said to them, "My food is to do the will of him who sent me and to accomplish his work. Do you not say, 'There are yet four months, then comes the harvest'? Look, I tell you, lift up your eyes, and see that the fields are white for harvest. Already the one who reaps is receiving wages and gathering fruit for eternal life, so that sower and reaper may rejoice together. For here the saying holds true, 'One sows and another reaps.' I sent you to reap that for which you did not labor. Others have labored, and you have entered into their labor." (John 4:34-38)

Keeping the great work of God at the forefront, we will look for ways to encourage and enable others to enter into this work. We read in Matthew 9:37-38: "Then he said to his disciples, 'The harvest is plentiful, but the laborers are few; therefore pray earnestly to the Lord of the harvest to send out laborers into his harvest.' "

Broaden the Field of Workers

We have already referenced Paul's instruction for church leaders "to equip the saints for the work of ministry, for building up the body of Christ" (Ephesians 4:12). A major reason for congregations becoming stagnant is because the preacher, elders, deacons or a few key members do everything and do not empower others to enter into the work. For example, if one lady teaches all of the classes for women or if one family plans all of the fellowship activities, there

> *A major reason for congregations becoming stagnant is because a few members do everything and do not empower others to enter the work.*

is a need to broaden the field of workers in these areas.

In the church, we need a group of workers sufficient for the long haul. If only one person can teach a Bible class, what will the congregation do if circumstances remove this teacher from the congregation? The work of God is so broad and so deep we can never have too many workers in the kingdom.

Congregations must also seek to include members of all ages in church work. We must honor and value the contribution of older members. Especially with the advances of health and wellness, men and women are remaining active well past what was considered the age of retirement. However, we must be mindful of making sure that younger Christians are also given an opportunity to serve.

I know of more than one congregation that, having once appointed elders, never appointed another man significantly younger than the existing elders. Perhaps these original men were in their 40s when they became elders. A decade later, they appoint a couple of new elders who are in their 50s. Another decade passes, and the new elders are in their 60s. Another decade passes, and they are in their 70s.

Congregations making these types of decisions are headed for trouble, as their elders become increasingly removed from the experiences of their younger members. The church must be conscious both to honor older members and to raise up new generations in the Lord's work.

Abounding Together in Faithfulness

Ira North closed his book *Balance* with a chapter titled "Let Us Remember What Is Required." He writes:

> God does not require that we be big, or wealthy, or powerful, or super smart. What our Heavenly Father requires is faithfulness. The important and absolutely essential thing is for us to be faithful. The apostle Paul teaches us that faithfulness is ours to plant and water and cultivate, but it is God's to give the increase. Let us not be too interested in numbers or bigness, but let us be vitally interested in faithfulness.

As we encourage one another in the work of the Lord, let us always keep this standard before us. Neil Anderson, the publisher of the *Gospel Advocate*, continues to encourage everyone who knows him with the words of Paul from 1 Corinthians 15:57-58: "But thanks be to God, who gives us the victory through our Lord Jesus Christ. Therefore, my beloved brothers, be steadfast, immovable, always

If we keep ourselves focused on Jesus, we will abound together in the work of the Lord.

abounding in the work of the Lord, knowing that in the Lord your labor is not in vain."

As we keep ourselves, our families and our congregations focused on Jesus, we will receive this victory and abound together in the work of the Lord.

For REFLECTION

1. *Can a person be a faithful Christian and not be a part of a congregation?*

2. *How can a congregation make sure and appropriately include members of all ages?*

3. *How can a congregation make sure to keep faithfulness as a priority?*

4. *How does preaching and teaching on eternal themes of heaven, hell and the day of judgment focus our attention on the need for effective service?*

NOTES: _____

_____

_____

_____

_____

_____

_____

_____

_____

_____

_____

_____

_____

_____

_____

_____

_____